Echoes Of Courage

Surviving Sexual Abuse and Rape

Asha Adira

Echoes of Courage: Surviving Sexual Abuse and Rape

Paperback ISBN: 978-1-957809-58-8
Hardcover ISBN: 978-1-957809-59-5

Published by Cornerstone Publishing

A Division of Cornerstone Creativity Group LLC
Info@thecornerstonepublishers.com
www.thecornerstonepublishers.com

Author's Contact

To book the author to speak at your next event or to order bulk copies of this book, please, use the information below:
ashaadira1@gmail.com

Printed in the United States of America.

CONTENTS

ACKNOWLEDGMENTS

This book is not exclusively the fruit of my pen but the outcome of a collaborative effort that enlightened my path and converted my words into a symphony of inspiration. I devote this book to those whose support, upliftment, and guidance helped construct these pages.

To my dearest husband, whose unswerving belief in me has been my rock throughout this process, your love, patience, and comprehension gave me the courage and motivation to continue. Your presence and encouragement have been a couple of the driving forces behind me putting pen to paper.

To my sincere friends who are the champions of my creativity, who never ceased to lend a listening ear, offered valuable insights, and pushed me to overcome my questioning, I am eternally grateful for your unwavering support and fueling my inner strength.

To my mentors, the guiding stars who kindly shared their intelligence and expertise, your constructive feedback, invaluable advice, and insightful critique have elevated this work beyond what I could have visualized.

My profound gratitude goes out to the esteemed scholars and experts. Your profound expertise and wisdom have empowered me to probe further into information that holds the potential to illuminate the understanding of parents, caregivers, or any reader intrigued by my story. Your invaluable guidance and assistance with evidence-based facts have been pivotal in shaping this book.The editors and publishing professionals who shaped my manuscript with sharp eyes, and diligent attention to detail, I appreciate you. Your commitment to refining my words while preserving my voice has metamorphosed this work into exactly what I imagined.

To my readers, the main destination of these words, who will embark on this literary journey with open minds and open hearts. Your willingness to capture my thoughts and experiences is why this book exists. It is for you that these pages were written, anticipating touching your lives in some meaningful way. The parents, guardians, and anyone who belongs to a community where children reside. Uncles, aunties, cousins, brothers, sisters, sisters-in-law, janitors, police officers, doctors, nurses, pastors, teachers, counselors, babysitters, influencers, community leaders, and everyone who has a relationship with or interacts with children.

I anticipate that this book will assist you in understanding what children who experience sexual abuse and rape encounter by me expressing incidents in my life of these encounters. May you do your part in protecting these innocent children, being their voice in the event of sexual abuse and rape.

May this acknowledgment testify to my gratitude for each of you. Without your passion, guidance, and support, this book would have remained but a dream. Thank you for believing in me, enlightening my way, and helping me bring my true story to life.

With limitless appreciation,
Asha Adira.

PREFACE

Often, I am asked why I have decided to share my story with the world, unravel the painful wounds beneath the surface, and enlighten the darkest corners of my past. The answer is super simple, yet profound-it is because I believe in the power of vulnerability, the power of healing, and the power of unfiltered truth. This book is a testament to the power of the spirit of humanity and the remarkable flexibility that resides within all of us. It is the raw narrative of my journey through the harrowing experiences of child abuse and rape, experiences that once threatened my silence forever.

For some time, the embarrassment and guilt associated with these traumas held me captive, fastened within the confines of my misery. I wore a mask, presenting the world with an illusion of normalcy, while my soul hollered in agony, yearning to break free from its chains.

But as I began to confront the pain and retrieve my voice, I uncovered that I was not alone. The darkness that once ate me alive was shared by countless others who had walked similar paths of anguish. And so, this book is also for those who have encountered unspeakable horrors, those who carry invisible scars, and those who believe that they are by themselves.

In this book, I give an unflinching account of the atrocities I endured, shedding light on the pit of despair that child abuse and rape can inflict upon a person's life. But this is not a story of victimhood; it is a story of survival, strength, and the unconquerable spirit that refuses to be extinguished.

I invite you, the reader, to journey alongside me as I drive the intricate web of trauma, healing, and transformation. As a unit, we will explore the recovery process, forgiveness's strength, and the human spirit's triumph. We will confront the difficult truths, challenge societal perceptions, highlight signs of child sexual abuse, grooming behaviors of perpetrators, and coping strategies, and brace the unyielding courage within us.

But let me be clear-this book is not just about me; it is about all the survivors who have fought to reclaim their lives, all the heroes who have emerged from the deepest pit of darkness to shine a light on others. It is a collective voice and a testament to the resilience of the human spirit.

So as you know, some of the incidents within these pages may not be easy to digest. They may evoke a series of emotions-anger, sadness and discomfort. I sincerely hope you will also find hope, strength, and the transformative power of healing through the tears and shadows. As we 'trod' this journey together, may we remember that our stories can crack the cycle of silence and light up long overdue conversations. As the light on child abuse and rape flickered, we could pave the way for understanding, empathy, and in the end, change.

Chapter One

Personal Account Of Surviving An Attack

As the door slammed shut, adrenaline coursed through my veins, instantly awakening my senses. My body responded rapidly to blood pressure and heart rate as if a flood of energy surged through every fiber of my being. In those intense moments, it felt as though my entire body had been engulfed by a torrent of blood, heightening my awareness to an almost overwhelming degree.

I stood frozen, my muscles tense, as if transformed into a statue, trapped in fear and uncertainty. The dryness that consumed my mouth was like wood chips parched under the scorching sun, a sensation that hinted at the internal turmoil raging inside me. It was as if a dormant fire had been lit in the depths of my being, fueling strange and unsettling energy that permeated my very aura. In that instant, I knew I was in grave danger.

He was of light complexion, and as the terrifying ordeal unfolded, I vividly remember the drastic transformation in his skin tone. Initially, his complexion appeared pink, perhaps due to his natural skin tone and the ambient lighting. However, as his sinister intentions became clear, his face flushed with anger, and his complexion turned red. How could a 15-year-old child turn him on?

He stood approximately five feet, eleven inches tall, possessing a medium build that hinted at a certain physical strength. A distinctive feature-his eye further accentuated his appearance. Behind his prescription glasses, his eyes appeared unusually protruding or 'pulped' out, creating a disturbing effect. It was as if his gaze carried a weight, a certain intensity that made me nervous.

He was dressed in a comfortable and lightweight white Merino, providing a sense of normalcy that sharply contrasted with the unsettling situation. His choice of clothing, while seemingly mundane, added to the paradox of the moment-a juxtaposition of everyday attire with the horrifying intent lurking beneath. A faded and 'washed out' plaid boxer peeked beneath his clothing. Though I did not pay close attention to its color, the worn appearance of the garment hinted at its age. Further, it contributed to the impression of a man disconnected from morality and decency.

My eyes locked onto him in sheer horror as the door slammed shut with a thunderous crash. Fear wrapped its suffocating arms around me, rendering me speechless and paralyzed. It was a heart-wrenching realization that this was merely an extension of the relentless torment I had already endured-a chilling repetition, this time with a different man.

His face twisted with an evil grin, sending shivers down my spine. A smile carried an undeniable discomfort, an eerie combination of malice and satisfaction. As he removed his glasses, a revelation unfolded before me-I could finally see his eyes, unobscured and exposed. They bore a disturbing intensity, brimming with what I now recognize as a twisted form of passion.

At that moment, the true nature of his desires became alarmingly clear. The gleam in his eyes, void of empathy or humanity, betrayed the depths of his perverted cravings.

The sight of his manhood shook me to the very core, imprinting itself upon my consciousness with a haunting permanence. In that moment of terrifying clarity, I understood that I was trapped in a twisted dance with another predator, an unwilling participant in a continuation of the horrors that had plagued my existence. The revelation intensified the fear that gripped me as I braced myself for the unthinkable, uncertain of the depths of darkness that awaited me.

The windows boasted a graceful French design featuring four rectangular panes. Despite their partial openness, hope for escape dwindled as the imposing burglar bars clung tightly to the window frames, rendering any passage impossible. Even if the windows had offered a path to freedom, my position near the bed made it clear that reaching them was an insurmountable task. The distance between myself and the window was too great, leaving me trapped within the confines of the room.

Across the room stood a brown wooden dressing table adorned with an assortment of bottles and objects used for personal hygiene. They held the potential to become a form of defense, a means to protect myself; however, they were out of reach. As I surveyed the room, a sense of impending doom settled upon me like a heavy shroud. The truth of my situation became painfully evident, overwhelming me with a feeling of helplessness. Once a place of comfort and refuge, the room has transformed into a prison.

On that day, I was absent from school, unable to attend due to an unfortunate turn of events. It began with the realization that my father, who usually provided me with lunch money, was unwell. His absence cast a shadow over our usual routine, leaving me without the means to meet my basic needs. In a challenging twist of circumstances, my aunt, who cared for the three of us, also faced financial constraints. She could not assist with her usual support and willingness to step in when needed.

Without viable options, I reluctantly remained at home while my cousins, whom I usually accompanied to school, pursued their educational endeavors. It was a day filled with a palpable sense of disappointment and a tinge of frustration as the circumstances conspired to keep me away from the learning environment which would have been my haven.

A horrifying wave crashed over me, sending tremors coursing through my body, rendering my legs weak and unsteady, as I noticed the protrusion of his manhood through his garment.

Intensity and fear consumed me, causing my heartbeat to reverberate so forcefully that I could almost envision its vibrations pulsating through my chest. In the deafening silence of the room, my panting breaths echoed like thunder, the sound magnified by the stillness around us. It was so quiet; you could hear the drop of a pin, a testament to the surreal suffocating atmosphere that had taken hold.

For an agonizing moment, he stood motionless, a haunting pause that seemed to stretch time itself. Every fiber of my being quivered as his gaze bore into me, his intentions menacingly clear. Petrified, I felt my trembling escalate, a rapid escalation of uncontrollable shivers. The question echoed with me, a desperate plea for answers: Why me: I had always been a humble, quiet, and obedient child, undeserving of such unspeakable horrors.

As he took those first steps toward me, my body became frozen, gripped by a paralyzing fear that rooted me to the spot. He seemed like he was in his late 40s and bore the marks of an avid beer drinker, his unhealthy gut serving as a visual testament to this. The resemblance to a pregnant woman in the latter stages of gestation is a disturbing image that further taints the sinister scene. I, an unassuming and dutiful child, had become entangled in a nightmare beyond understanding.

Tainted with the foul odor of fish, his breath assaulted my senses as he forcefully pressed his angry, sinful face closer to mine. Despite being consumed with terror, I obeyed the instinctive mandate ingrained in me, opening my mouth as wide as a shark's, ready to sink my teeth into any part of his face within reach. Our lips collided, and I grabbed one of his between my teeth, clenching it tightly. In a momentary pause, he recoiled, uttering an expletive that described me as if I were the transgressor. My heart raced, thunderous beats threatening to escape through my quivering lips.

With both my arms painfully extended and pinned down by his own, I was trapped in a vulnerable 'butterfly' position on the bed. A creeping sensation of dead washed over me as I felt his unyielding 'iron' slowly rubbing against my most private area. His waist gyrated in a circular motion, mimicking the dancers' movements at a soca party, a disgusting display of pleasure that sent revulsion down my spine. Each time I attempted to scream, my voice was stifled by my breath as he employed his mouth over mine, attempting to force a kiss upon me.

As I continued to resist, it became evident that I

was fighting for my dignity and survival. Pinned flat on my back, captured by the weight of his body, each passing moment felt like an eternity of torment. He released his hold on one of my hands, only to reveal his disgusting manhood. It loomed before me, resembling the enormous plantains my grandmother used to cultivate in the backyard. In that harrowing instant, the specter of death itself stared me in the face, casting a shadow over any remnants of hope.

As he shifted his body weight and attempted to access his private parts, I mustered every ounce of strength and unleashed a forceful kick in his direction. The impact disrupted his assault for a second, but he quickly retaliated by exerting the full pressure of his midsection onto my defenseless body. With 'a free hand,' he brazenly lifted my skirt, attempting to remove my underwear. Immediately a destructive power seemed to possess me. Fueled by some spiritual energy, I sank my fingers deep into his eyes, unleashing a torrent of pain upon him.

He screamed so loudly through the room walls, echoing with a twisted sense of victimhood as if he were the one being assaulted. He bellowed, accusing me of attempting to blind him, his words laced with self-pity and sorrow. Yes, I thought bitterly; that was my intention. The heat of anger radiated through my body, my emotions swirling into a feverish storm. Tears streamed down my face, a testament to an overwhelming flood of emotions that threatened to consume me, yet I clenched my teeth.

With each passing moment, his once imposing body weight began to subside, his strength diminishing. I continued to kick, the force of my defiance surging as his power faced me. The more he faltered, the more my strength seemed to grow; my warrior spirit was awakened. Eventually, he accepted defeat, retreating from the room in anger, spewing expletives that echoed in the air.

I found myself sitting on the bed, surrounded by chaos. The absence of a safety lock on the door meant I could not fortify myself at this moment. I desperately hoped that he would not come back. But now, a fierce determination burned in my eyes, ready to confront any challenge.

The living room was filled with a symphony of sounds: the rustling of bags and furniture shifting. Simultaneously, the distinctive clatter of the burglar bars resonated through the air, signaling the intruder's departure from the premises. In a split second, my body reacted, propelling me off the bed with lightning speed. I forcefully shut the living room door, sealing off the path to the verandah. My heart raced, its wild beats echoing the adrenaline gushing through my veins.

I sank into the sofa, desperately trying to gather my thoughts. My mind spun in disarray, overwhelmed by terror, leaving me feeling bewildered. Tears flowed down my cheeks, and I succumbed to uncontrollable sobs. Questions raced through my mind like a hurricane, questioning the reasons behind my unfortunate experiences. An intense burning sensation overtook my entire being like my skin had been coated in fiery cayenne pepper. The reflection of myself in the mirror resembled someone a wild savage beast tackled. At that moment, I could not help but see myself as a vulnerable little girl caught in a world far too cruel.

Chapter Two

Unveiling The Unending Narrative

This man was the very same one who worked for a government agency and had been granted permission by my caregiver to stay overnight on occasion. It was a disturbing truth that he would summon me to join him in bed while my aunt took her nightly showers. My caregiver ran a business for one of her friends or perhaps even her friend's husband. The details of the man's other business ventures remained elusive, leaving me uncertain why he could not operate his enterprise. My caregiver often returned home late, typically after 10 p.m. During these visits, he would reach out to me, summoning my presence.

I found peace when my aunt finally found a man who genuinely cared about me. He exuded warmth and kindness, showing a sincere interest in my life. He would often inquire about my teachers, friends at school, and neighbors who had become close companions. He seemed genuinely curious about everyone I knew, creating an atmosphere of pure connection.

During each visit, he would continue asking me to join him in bed. During one of these encounters, he noticed my lack of a computer and promised to rectify that. "Every little girl should have a computer," he said. His intentions seemed noble; he believed it would assist me with my school assignments and be a resource I would share with my friends. Owning a computer held great significance during that time, as it was a luxury that only a few children would afford. In my corner of the world, we had not fully embraced the computer age yet, making the prospect of having one even more extraordinary.

The prospect of becoming a part-time computer programmer filled me with great enthusiasm, and having a brand-new computer would undoubtedly facilitate my aspirations. I held a deep passion for computer science, and my fondness for my computer science teacher at school only intensified my interest in the field. These experiences ignited a growing sense of trust, gradually strengthening my connection with him as he groomed me.

As weeks passed, his comfort level with me in bed during our nighttime encounters when my aunt went to take her showers seemed to increase. He became increasingly playful, offering warm hugs that felt comforting and authentic. These embrace evoked a family sense of goodness, reminiscent of the affectionate hugs I had received from the men in my family, particularly my grandfather, before he passed away. My grandfather stood as the embodiment of love and protection in my life. His unwavering affection knew no bounds, and he would go to great lengths to safeguard me from any harm or danger.

After several weeks, the promised computer failed to materialize. He said the delay was due to a challenge with the seller, prolonging my eagerness. Although I was waiting forever, it seemed, my excitement remained undebated, and I eagerly entered the room without hesitation whenever my caregiver stepped away, answering his calls. However, as our relationship grew more comfortable, these encounters began to take a distressing turn, becoming increasingly unsettling and invasive, crossing boundaries, leaving me feeling uneasy, vulnerable, and questioning his true intentions.

He began pulling the sheets over us, and I felt uneasy, sensing something was amiss. Despite the growing discomfort, he had established trust within me, and the desire for the promised computer intensified. Fear gripped me as I was terrified of angering him and jeopardizing my opportunity to obtain the coveted device.

He noted my evident discomfort and tried to quell my fears by urging me to 'relax,' assuring me that his intentions were not to harm me. However, despite his hollow words, his actions only intensified my unease. He was determined to touch my breasts, his hands violating the boundaries of my body while pulling me closer to him. Instructing me to lie with my back turned away from his face, he sought to assert control and dominance over me in the most invasive manner. At times I felt his hard manhood rubbing against my bottom. Shock and confusion overwhelmed my young mind as I grappled with the gravity of the situation unfolding before me.

These distressing encounters repeated themselves a few more times, each instance leaving an indelible mark on my psyche. The nights became a haunting cycle of dread and desperation as I devised a strategy to protect myself. Determined to avoid his clutches, I sought refuge in the kitchen, biding my time until the sounds of the shower signaled my caregiver's presence again. His voice calling my name became a chilling reminder of the darkness I had been subjected to.

Questions plagued my thoughts, consuming me with their weight. Was this the twisted motivation behind his attempt to rape me? Had he lured me in the promise of a computer, using it as a tool to exploit my trust? The realization struck me with a sickening jolt as I grappled with the betrayal and realized that the safety I thought I had found had been shattered.

Chapter Three

Untold Agony-The Unseen Suffering Child

As I followed him through the winding path, my senses were heightened to the slightest movement and sound. With each step, my heart raced like a wind stallion, threatening to break free from my chest. The air was thick with humidity, causing my skin to glisten with beads of sweat. I took in the scent of the earthly soil beneath my feet and the sweet aroma of the flowers that lined the path. As we approached the porch, the chirping of crickets and rustling of leaves filled my ears. I could see the faint glimmer of peenie wallie, twinkling like fairy lights in the darkness. A dense wall of bushes partially hid the porch itself, their shadows looming in the dim light of the evening.

My 'guide' paused, facing me with a smoldering intensity in his eyes. The combination of the shadows and the low light made it difficult to read his expression, but his gaze was unmistakable. He extended his hand and reached for my hand, and I felt a jolt of electricity course through me as our fingers intertwined with a little bit of aggression. I followed him because earlier in the evening, he agreed to assist me with my science project due the next day at the low wall fence separating his walkway from my yard. He had helped me with a few projects, which was nothing new.

I always saw him as the 'good neighbor' because his dad was our close family friend. My caregiver sometimes cooked food and shared it with him, and I was the food delivery person. Their home was in the back of a large house, and it was sectioned off like an apartment, with four families living there, including him and his dad.

He was tall, towering above me at around six feet, and while I was not entirely sure of his age, I guessed he was around 22. At the time, I had just turned 14. As he continued to hold my hand and we walked, I noticed we passed the steps leading to the porch, where we sat to work on projects. Other times we had sat outside in a weathered wooded chair in his part of the yard. But this time, he led me past those familiar spots.

I could see the flickering light of a TV through the windows on the porch, signaling that his dad was likely home. Despite feeling apprehensive, I followed him anyway. I knew that project was now on the back burner, but I stayed silent because my self-esteem was very low, and I was almost afraid of everything. As we continued deeper into the back of the house, I could not shake an uneasy feeling, wondering where he was taking me and what we would do.

"Where are we going?" I asked hesitantly, hoping he would ease my suspicions. Despite my apprehension, he pulled me along, growing more insistent with each step we took. My heart pounded faster and faster in my chest as he led me towards the bushes, the darkness enveloping us with each passing moment. The closer we got to the bushes, the more I resisted his advances, but the tighter he held on, leaving me trapped and vulnerable. The further in the bushes we went, the only sound I could hear was the rustling of our steps on the crispy banana leaves spread across the ground. I tried to wiggle my hand out of his grip, but it was too tight; he kept tugging me. With every step, my heart pounded harder and faster than before. The more he pulled me forward, the more petrified I became, feeling my breaths shallower and more constricted with every step. The silence was so thick that the only sound I could hear was the galloping of my heart in my ears, fueling my growing fear of where we were headed.

As I gazed into the night, the twinkling lights of the nearby telephone company caught my attention. Peering through the dense foliage, the tiny luminescent orbs resembled stars scattered in the dark abyss. Suddenly, a strikingly vivid white object caught my eyes, a radiant sheet of an oversized blanket lying on the ground. My heart continued to race as he lifted my skirt and violently tugged at my underwear. His overpowering strength left me completely defenseless, with no energy to find him off any longer. This segment of the assault continued for what felt like an excruciatingly long two minutes as tears uncontrollably streamed down my face. My once-lively limbs now felt like lifeless appendages, my body surrendering to the unspeakable violation.

While I lay there, feeling small and lifeless beneath him, he thrust what felt like an immense member into my tiny vaginal opening. At that moment, a striking image emerged in my mind's eyes-the visage of Jesus Christ crucified on the cross. This was the same Christ that had been depicted to me as a defender of the innocent, but I felt no protection now. Before he passed, my grandfather used to sing a song with the words 'Suffer the little children to come unto me. And I will redeem them and hold them close to my bosom.' This was the voice of Jesus, suggesting that he would protect little children.

I was struck silent, overwhelmed by the violation occurring to me. My mouth hung unmoved, my tears forming a steady stream down the sides of my face as he thrust himself into me with brutal force. The feeling of suffocation overwhelmed me as my nose became congested and my breathing labored. He did not seem to notice or care. He did not seem to care as he continued his rough movements, and his grunts sounded like those of a wild feral beast. The intensity of these thrusts made my gag reflects kick in, and my body convulsed with pain, but he showed no mercy. As he approached his climax, his grunting became deeper and deeper and more fervent until, finally, his body tensed, and he collapsed onto me like a lifeless heavyweight.

As I lay there, exposed, and weakened, my once thriving world crumbled around me. My spirit was crushed, and my strength evaporated. Each breath seemed to be a battle, every pulse a fight to stay alive. The familiar sense of security I had always found in my surroundings was stripped away in a moment of betrayal. The powerlessness and vulnerability I felt made me wish for an escape, for the earth to swallow me alive, just like it had done to my grandfather. Yet, as I tried to gather the remnants of myself and clumsily rise to my feet, the harsh reality of my situation became even starker. I felt worthless, as though I was nothing more than an object for his pleasure. I was so insecure and unprotected that my existence felt like a burden, an unwanted weight I carried wherever I went. As I got up, the sound of his metal belt buckles jingled, mocking me with its sinister tone.

As I mustered the strength to distance myself from him, my steps carried me forward, propelled by determination and despair. He let me go, releasing me as though my worth did not worth the effort of holding onto. With each stumbling stride, my legs felt burdened, weighed by an invisible heaviness that threatened to topple me at any moment. Amid the turmoil within me, my thoughts and emotions became a zig-zag puzzle, their pieces scattered and unrecognizable. A numbing sensation overtook my entire being, rendering me detached from the sensations that should have permeated my existence. In that disorienting moment, I found myself grappling with the unsettling question of whether I was still capable of experiencing any feeling at all.

The walk home was a blur, my surroundings a sea of vague shapes and colors. All I could hear was the thump of my heartbeat which rolled like thunder in my ears, a constant reminder of the harrowing events that had unfolded. I struggled to remember how I made my way home but eventually found alone in the room I shared with my cousin. The weight of being alone pressed upon me, casting doubt on whether I would ever regain familiarity with myself. Questions were like a whirlwind as I asked myself, 'Will I ever be the same again?'

The icy touch of the water sent shivers down my spine, each droplet feeling like a sharp needle piercing my skin. At that moment, the overwhelming urge swept over me, a desperate longing to rid myself of this physical vessel, shed it like a worn-out shell, and consign it to the flames of an imagined fire pit. I crawled into the shower and vigorously lathered and scrubbed my body, driven by an intense desire to rid myself of the heavyweight that burdened my soul. With each forceful stroke, my skin felt pure agony, like it dissolved in an acid wash. The burning pain seared through me, reminiscent of the sharp sting of a freshly inflicted wound sprinkled with fiery pepper.

As I gazed down the drain, I saw a mixture of water tainted with a light shade of red and bubbles, an unsettling sight. Tears streamed down my face as I relentlessly forced the washcloth upon my 'flesh.' A profound sense of numbness washed over my vulva as if carrying the weight of a heavy burden, stifling the essence of my femininity. It felt like an invisible force was constricting, suffocating my womanhood's soft core. The sensation of being trapped, unable to breathe freely, cast a shadow over my sense of self, leaving me disconnected from my femininity's innate power and beauty.

Instantly, a loud and sudden bang almost shattered the bathroom door. Startled, my heart beat fast again as I heard my cousin's voice on the other side. Her concern was palpable, and I could tell she was worried. She was my loyal companion, and I was hers for as long as I could remember. Our playtime and responsibilities often overlapped as we grew up together as siblings would. I took a deep breath, trying to keep my composure, answering her in a shaky voice. But the truth was, I was struggling to stand up straight. The world seemed to spin around me as I felt weak and helpless. My body felt heavy, as if it were freezing in time.

My cousin was justifiably impatient as she questioned me again, 'What are you doing that is taking so long?' Trying to sound reassuring, I whispered, 'I am getting out soon.' But my breath was short, and my mind was racing. I felt the weight of my struggles bearing down on me and was desperate for it to disappear as if it were an inanimate object that could be evaded with a simple twist of fate. As I stood quivering in the bathroom, I could not help but realize how dependent we were on each other. We were two young souls trying to navigate a big world that was often unpredictable and tough. We needed each other's help, empathy, and trust. At that moment, as I struggled to summon the courage to face the world, I could not have felt more grateful for having my cousin by my side.

I remember those dreadful moments-they seemed to happen more often than not. Each instance was marked by a sense of coercion that clung to me like a suffocating mist. Some weeks it would happen once; other weeks, twice or even thrice. As time passed, weeks melded into months, and months blended into a year. Each time, I would cringe inside, or other times, too intimidated to stay in, I would venture out into my world, heart pounding and anxious. The fear of what might come next always lurked at the top of my mind. Could it have gotten any worse? It was a truly harrowing experience.

He told me that neither my caregiver nor his dad would believe me because of their close relationship. Firstly, my caregiver would have disbelieved, and because she did, his dad would have automatically disbelieved if I uttered anything about my experience with him. I felt a crushing blow to my self-assurance. The idea of being disbelieved left me feeling powerless and exposed. Gradually, I became more introverted, apprehensive, and malleable to the opinions of others. My self-worth sunk, and I was constantly wracked by nervousness and unease.

I occasionally brought food to his father in the evenings after my cousin, and I had prepared it. My giver at work at the bar usually gave this order and did not return home until late at night. Upon arriving, I often found his dad sitting on his couch, engrossed in watching TV. However, there was one evening when things took a disturbing turn. As I entered the house, his dad introduced me to a pornography film on TV. I nervously placed the food down on the dinner table while feeling a sense of discomfort wash around me. Although his dad invited me to stay,

I declined and quickly fled the house. It was clear that the perversion I was experiencing from his son had been learned from his dad or possibly in their generation.

I remember vividly, as a young and innocent girl of only six or seven years old, the first time I experienced sexual abuse. It was not a dramatic moment like Russ holding me down in a room, Bunny who terrorized and exploited me, or my neighbor who repeatedly raped me. Instead, it was a slow and insidious invasion of my body and mind perpetrated by someone who was meant to protect me. Our caregiver asked him to accompany us to the Christmas concert in the street. What was Joy to the World for everyone in the crowd that night was sadness and discomfort for me. I was too small to see the stage from the ground, so George lifted me and placed me on his neck, with me wearing my fancy polka dot dress. He used one of his hands to access my private part and fondled it most of the night in the middle of the crowded park. At that moment, I could not fully understand the nature of what had happened, but I knew deep within it was far from being right. It began an intense breach of trust and safety that would forever shape my identity as a survivor. It was an unsettling experience that shattered my innocence and introduced me to the world's harsh realities.

Chapter Four

The Brush With Danger

As whispers of his demise spread, news of a fatal gunshot that struck him in the head while he sat in his car in bustling Kingston city, a strange sentiment overcame me. There was a sense of jubilation in my heart. I remained detached, devoid of any emotional reaction, as the announcement of his murder reached my ears. It was as if a shield had enveloped my innermost self, rendering me unfeeling and distant from the event unfolding. However, beneath the surface, the scars he had inflicted upon me were deeply embedded, appalling reminders of the pain he had caused my very being.

A profound absence of sympathy gripped me, extending toward him and his loved ones. In my eyes, the magnitude of the emotional and mental torment he had subjected me seemed impossible. It was as if I had assumed the role of the judge in my thoughts, grappling with the overwhelming weight of the suffering he had inflicted upon me. He belonged to the ranks of those who played a role in dismantling my adolescence, callously robbing me of my once cherished sense of innocence. The scars left behind were a testament to his profound impact on shaping my life.

Standing approximately five feet tall, he possessed a dark brown complexion that lent an air of mystery to his presence. His typical attire consisted of snug-fitting skinny jeans and silk shirts, accentuating his unique style. However, his physical appearance was characterized by an abdomen that protruded noticeably, as if he were an avid beer drinker. His shirt clung tightly to his bulging midsection, creating a visual contrast that could not be ignored. Completing his ensemble were boots reminiscent of classic Western movies, boasting pointed toes and a modest two-or three-inch heel. His preferred footwear consisted of a distinctive pair of brown shoes adorned with intricate patterns of tiny dots. These dots appeared meticulously sewn into the material, creating a textured surface with raised dots of threads. He consistently presented himself well-groomed with a keen eye for fashion, paying careful attention to this appearance. The lingering fragrance of his cologne was potent, its intensity capable of overwhelming even those who had lost their sense of smell, penetrated the air and left a lasting impression.

Rarely did a smile grace his lips as if the world's weight rested heavily upon his shoulders. He carried himself with an air of self-assuredness, walking with his head held high and a subtle bounce to his step, almost as if he tiptoed through life. The duration of his stay remains blurry in my memory, but his impact on our household during that time was nothing short of terrifying and deeply disturbing. It marked the most harrowing and traumatic chapters of living under the same roof as someone who inflicted such fear and anguish upon us.

During his presence in our household, the true extent of his deceitfulness gradually unraveled before my eyes. Insomnia plagued me relentlessly, and it was only in moments of sheer exhaustion that sleep reluctantly embraced me. Nightmares haunted my nights, their vividness blurring the line between imagination and reality. In those harrowing dreams, my senses awakened with alarming clarity, amplifying the fear that gripped me. Persistent anxiety and debilitating headaches became my unwelcome companions, lingering daily. Even when the throbbing pain impaired my vision, I pushed myself to attend school, for the thought of being confined within the house with him during the daylight hours was too much to bear. Witnessing the secret of life he led in shadows, a pervasive belief took hold in my young mind that one day, something terrible would happen, brought about by evil people. Fear clung to me like a constant shadow that never left my side, intensifying whenever he was in the house.

"Smell this," he taunted, forcefully thrusting his fingers toward Kim's nose. We stood together in the passageway, consumed by fear of his presence. "This is Donna's private part." Kim, who was two years older than me, possibly sixteen years old back then, shared the same terror I felt. Donna was also a relative by blood about a year older than Kim. She would visit us on weekends and occasionally join us for longer periods, such as summer vacations and Christmas holidays.

Our bond was very strong within this segment of our family circle; we were deeply connected. The tension in our household was noticeable, and it hung heavy in the air. Our caregiver, who worked at a restaurant and bar, was absent, leaving us alone with the predator. I was aware that he subjected Kim and Donna to abuse, but the knowledge remained buried in the recesses of my mind. I was too frightened to talk with them about it, just as I believed they were hesitant to disclose anything. Occasionally, I could sense fragments of conversation being exchanged between them, snippets of information being shared, though it was scarce and elusive.

The day he entered our lives, a shift occurred, seemingly for the better. He showered us with many treats, flooding our days with ice cream, delicious fruit cake, and extravagant dinners. Jerked chicken and fish became a regular occurrence, dishes that held a certain rarity and price tag in the place I called home. In my culture, such meals were reserved for special occasions, yet here we indulged in them almost daily, courtesy of the person who would later reveal his monstrous nature. The taste of a popular fried chicken on our lips became synonymous with finger-licking delight, a guilty pleasure that momentarily masked the darkness lurking beneath. He did not hesitate to give us generous sums of five hundred dollars as our 'pocket money.' This seemingly abundant amount served as a safety net in case our lunch funds ran dry or we desired to indulge in extra treats during school hours. Although my father faithfully provided me with daily lunch money for the most part, the additional cash made me feel wealthy. I sometimes utilized my newfound wealth to purchase food for my friends who had nothing to eat. While our family was not affluent, we enjoyed a comfortable lifestyle. He would inquire about our aspirations and dreams for adulthood, engaging us in conversations that feigned genuine interest in our lives.

As days turned into weeks, an undeniable decline began to creep into our household. I could not pinpoint the exact cause, but I could sense that it stemmed from the troubles plaguing the adults. His presence became increasingly scarce within our walls as he ventured out more frequently, disappearing into the night. His appetite waned, as he rarely partook in meals at home.

The visits from his friends, son, and cousin became increasingly infrequent, almost nonexistent. His son, a young man who resided just a few houses down the street, would occasionally drop by to converse with his father on the verandah. However, even those interactions became rare. His cousin, who lived in another city, used to visit on certain Saturdays but now seemed to have vanished without a trace. The façade of goodness he once maintained in the presence of my caregiver, and the rest of us crumbled. He grew sullen and withdrawn, his silence casting a heavy shadow over our interactions. The once lively conversations among the adults dwindled, leaving strained silence.

On the days when my cousin Kim chose not to attend school, she would retreat to the safety of the front or guest room, hiding beneath the bed. It was her sanctuary while he slumbered in the back room designated for the grown-ups. She remained hidden under the bed, enduring the passing hours in solitude, until the comforting presence of someone else arrived at home. In the confined space beneath the bed, she sought solace and protection from the lurking darkness that permeated the household.

Unbeknownst to him, Kim would remain hidden under the bed, enduring hunger throughout the day, determined to evade a potential confrontation with him. Only long after his untimely demise did Kim reveal this secret to me. Most nights, he would venture out, disappearing in the darkness until the early morning hours or sometimes even until the break of dawn, just before we prepared to leave for school. I naively believed that he was attending live parties, as our culture was known for its vibrant and frequent social gatherings that spanned every night of the week.

One fateful morning, as I walked through the passageway toward the bathroom, I noticed him casually tossing a white T-shirt onto my caregiver's bed. It was an ordinary act, or so I thought. However, to my astonishment, a large, menacing black gun tumbled out from its folds as the shirt landed on the mattress. My heart skipped a beat as fear coursed through my veins, freezing me in place. It was a startling and chilling sight, disturbing my peace of that early morning hour. I knew that was not a legal gun.

Thankfully, he had not noticed my presence as his back was turned towards the doorway. Swiftly, I hurried into the safety of the bathroom, seeking refuge from the unnerving sight that had unfolded before my eyes. My heart raced so intensely that it felt like it might leap out of my chest. The pounding in my ears matched the rhythm of my frantic pulse, while a dizzying sensation overwhelmed me as if my blood pressure had skyrocketed in an instant. I was very intimidated by him. I was overcome with disarray, my thoughts scattered like puzzle pieces, as the realization of the heaviness of the situation settled upon me. With his nightly absences, my mind became a breeding ground for the most disturbing and sinister imaginings. Fear coiled around me, tightening its grip with each passing moment. The memory of who else was in the house at the time eludes me as my focus becomes consumed by the weight of that revelation. From that day forward, a profound shift occurred within me, transforming my aura into a constant state of anxiety.

"Come and feel this. Come and suck it." His words hung in the air, a grotesque invitation that froze me in place, holding the tray with trembling hands. He rested his plate on the tray, adorned with a savory dish of curried cabbage and sauteed in aromatic herbs accompanied by bread. It became apparent that this was his favorite breakfast, a menu that catered to his indulgence. We served him his meals in bed, treating him as the self-proclaimed king of our household. Despite our tender years, my cousin and I honed our culinary skills, preparing delectable dishes that tantalized our taste buds.

It was an imposing sight, commanding attention with its huge size and unyielding hardness. He held it firmly, his fingers coiling around its girth as he casually swiveled it in his hand, leisurely reclining on the bed. The moment's weight hung heavily in the room, an uncomfortable tension filling the air as I stood frozen, my gaze was involuntarily drawn to the spectacle before me, and time seemed to stand still as I struggled to understand the gravity of the situation, my mind racing with a mixture of fear, confusion, and disgust.

At that moment, my senses heightened, and the weight of the situation pressed upon me like a suffocating force. The memory of the gun, and its ominous presence, flooded my mind, intertwining with the current scenes before the meme. The long black body part he now held seemed to echo the shape and darkness of that weapon, intensifying my unease. My hands trembled uncontrollably, causing the tray to shudder in my grasp. Conflicting thoughts raced through my mind as I felt tension with the overwhelming fear and uncertainty.

Should I abandon the tray and flee, seeking safety from the looming danger? Should I cautiously turn around, hoping to blend into the background and avoid drawing more attention? Should I obediently comply with his disturbing request, succumbing to the power he seemed to wield over me? The questions swirled in a chaotic whirlwind, leaving me paralyzed with indecision. Time seemed to both stretch and compress, each passing second a harsh reminder of the choices I had to make.

My instincts urged me to protect myself and

prioritize my well-being above all else. But the fear of his potential anger and reprisal lingered, casting a shadow of doubt upon my every move. Should I risk provoking him further or bide my time, waiting for the opportunity to escape this situation? The internal struggle consumed me, boosting the vulnerability I was experiencing at that very moment.

As I stood there, the tray trembling in my hands, I became aware of the delicacy of my existence, trapped in a web of his power and dominance. The room felt suffocating, the air thick with tension, and I yearned for a flicker of guidance, a silver of courage to guide me through the darkness that surrounded me.

Despite the fear and uncertainty coursing through my veins, I summoned the courage to maintain my composure. Taking a deep breath to steady myself, I firmly responded, "No." It felt like time stood still in the moment as I resisted the powerful grip of fear and asserted my boundaries. Placing the tray on the bed slowly, I slowly turned and walked away, my heart pounding. Leaving the room, a sense of relief washed over me mingled with profound gratitude. It felt like an unseen force intervened, protecting me from the evil of this tyrant who always seemed to get what he wanted. The realization dawned upon me that perhaps I had been saved by a higher power or the strength within myself that I had yet to comprehend fully.

In the aftermath of this chilling encounter, my appetite vanished. The once inviting aroma of the food seemed tainted by the menacing presence that loomed over our household. Hastily, I dressed in my school uniform, my hands shaking slightly as I hastily buttoned my shirt and adjusted my tie. With dismay and determination, I went through the gate, leaving the oppressive atmosphere behind me.

Walking towards the school, the world seemed both familiar and foreign. The weight of what had transpired lingered in the back of my mind, casting a shadow over the unusual routines of the day. Thoughts raced through my head, questioning why such gloom had invaded our lives and how we could find solace and safety amidst the chaos. As I ventured further into the school, the gates offered a reprieve, providing a sense of normalcy from the horrifying reality that possibly awaited my return.

I held onto a glimmer of hope in the depths of my being, believing that there was a force greater than the scary events that plagued our lives. I made a silent pact with myself, promising to preserve, seek out the strength within, and protect myself and those I cared about. While the scars of these experiences may have left their mark, they also ignited resilience, a resolve to rise above the darkness and reclaim our lives.

Walking closer to the classroom, my steps carried a newfound determination. I yearned for knowledge and sought refuge within the halls of education, where the pursuit of understanding and growth provided comfort. I knew that education would be my ticket to liberation, my means of escaping the clutches of this oppressive existence.

Though the road ahead remained daunting with each passing day, I would strive to build a better future for myself and others who had suffered silently, their voices muffled by fear and shame. I vowed to break the chains that bound us, to amplify our collective voices, and to seek justice and healing for all who endured the horrors of child sexual abuse.

As I walked away from the room tainted by the tyrant's presence, I carried a newfound strength in that pivotal moment. It was a testament to the human spirit's resilience, a refusal to succumb to the darkness that threatened us. And so, with unwavering determination, I continued my journey towards a brighter tomorrow, guided by the unwavering belief that love, courage, and justice prevail would prevail.

Chapter Five

Against My Will-The 'Threesome' I Escaped

As I curiously peeked through the window, I spotted a woman outside. My nosey tendencies always led me to check who was at the gate whenever there was some commotion outside. She appeared to be a fair-skinned Asian woman, no younger than 40, holding a cigarette. She had a skinny frame weighing no more than 120 lbs and was 5 feet 3 inches tall. She was accompanied by a couple of other people and the tyrant that evoked a grip of fear who lived with us at the time.

She walked in the door accompanied by the devil.

Chiney, as she was called, had come over on a pleasant Saturday evening. This was the second time I had seen her a few weeks prior; she had come by but had remained at the gate. But today, she was inside and settling in for a visit.

She gave a gracious smile and softly said, 'come sit right here.' As I approached the couch, I noticed they had both shifted to opposite ends, leaving ample space in the center for me to settle in comfortably. As I nestled in between them, the soft glow of the evening sunlight pouring in through the window illuminated the room, casting a warm and calming ambiance. Sitting in their presence, I could feel my nerves and confusion mounting. Though she appeared to be a kind and gentle soul, I could not shake the feeling that she was somehow connected to the darkness lurking in my past. The television was airing the latest sports news, the commentator's voice enveloping the room like a cozy blanket. As I looked around the room, a thought crossed my mind. I realized my caregiver was working hard, holding down the fort for her boss, who owned the bustling bar.

I could not help but notice the 'bang' adorning Chiney's forehead, complementing her captivating smile. She reminded me of the elegant Asian ladies I had seen on the silver screen, dressed in short skirt that showed off her petite legs and high heels that resembled those of exotic dancers. As we sat shoulder to shoulder in the cramped space, I had to squeeze myself into the gap forcefully. Why did they want a little girl sitting between them? I had been violated so many times, so no doubt, my nerves were becoming evident. Despite the discomfort, neither Chiney nor her companion, my dreaded nightmare, tried to bulge to give me some room. We were tightly packed like a small sardine can, struggling to find our own space.

It was a strange and uncomfortable situation when Chiney suddenly put her arm around my neck in a tight embrace. Her compliments about my looks and body only added to my unease. With my cousins away on holiday, it was just me and the two adults in the room. Then, she placed her hand on my breast, and my fear skyrocketed. The fact that Bunny was also there only exacerbated the feeling of danger. It was a terrifying experience and something that will stay with me for a long time to come.

'Nice stiff breasts,' Chiney uttered. 'It would be nice to suck them.' *They are about to finish me off this evening,* I thought. I felt her hand slip into my blouse, pushing further into my bra and stroking my breast. But instead of pleasure,

I felt a sharp pain radiating from the touch. It was even a particularly tight grip, but for some reason, it hurt terribly. It might have been the terror I felt at the time. It was confusing and unsettling, leaving me unsure of how to respond. These sensations stayed with me for some time, lingering long after the encounter ended. I know now that it violated my boundaries, but I was left feeling uncomfortable.

I felt completely powerless, consumed by fear and desperation. The horror of being raped, although not a new experience, drowned my mind. Prayers poured out of me, begging for mercy. I could not believe this was happening- the threat of a threesome looming over me like a nightmare. Bunny was just grinning like it was all some kind of sick joke, enjoying the trauma he was causing me. His squinted eyes would not leave us like he relished every moment of this sick game. It was difficult to explain my feelings at that moment-violated, traumatized, deeply disgusted. And yet, even as I write about it now, the raw memories and emotions of that experience are still so palpable. It is a moment that has forever changed me, and I will never forget how it felt to be so powerless in the face of such cruel manipulation.

Normally I am not the one to back down from

a fight, but I felt completely defeated then. It is hard to describe, but I felt like I had already given up-like I was already dead. And then, as if by some miracle, a man came and called Bunny outside. At first, I did not know what to make of it-was it all a part of some sick plan? But as I listened to their conversation, I realized it was the nearby mechanic. At that moment, I felt a glimmer of hope. Maybe this was my chance to escape Bunny and the nightmare he was subjecting me to. But even as I talked to the higher power in me, I could not shake the feeling that there was something more to this. Something sinister, something dangerous.

As I sat there, staring at the grey Toyota Corolla parked outside the gate through the crack of the door, my heart raced with fear and adrenaline. I knew the culprit was responsible for the unsettling events of the evening in the house. Minutes passed, and my resolve grew stronger as I reached a decision. Without hesitation, I walked away swiftly, pushed the gate open, and zapped towards my neighbor's house, seeking solace and a few moments of peace.

Sitting in my neighbor's cozy living room, I could not help but think about the stranger lurking in my house and the barbaric animal who orchestrated it all. My nerves tingled; I checked the time, thinking of my caregiver, hoping she would return soon. I needed some form of protection, some assurance that everything would be alright. But as the night drifted by, I caught between fear and hope. It is one moment that I will never fully understand but does not need to be understood, as plans they had for me were redirected because of the mechanic next door.

Chapter Six

Darkness Descends

In the dark recesses of my soul, the outsiders' violation penetrated with a force that surpassed mere physical contact. It infiltrated the innermost chambers of my being, reaching depths where vulnerability and innocence thrived. Like merciless intruders, their actions tore through the protective layers that should have shielded my sense of self, leaving an indelible scar that would forever redefine the trajectory of my existence. The sanctity I once held dear, the belief that my body and boundaries were sacred, was shattered into countless fragments. It was a violation that defined understanding, for it went beyond the physical acts inflicted upon me. It was an assault on my very essence, an assault that disrupted the delicate equilibrium of my identity, leaving me grasping at the fragments of the person I once knew myself to be.

In the aftermath of their transgressions, the echoes of their actions haunted the corridors of my memories, consistently reminding me of the horror I endured. Like a haunting refrain, their presence lingered, weaving itself into the fabric of my consciousness, unable to ignore or escape. It was a non-stop chaos that played on, forever imprinted on a huge part of my life story. Along the line of my memory, I fought pain, confusion, and the delicate balance between reclaiming control and succumbing to the weight of their violation. Once filled with memories of my early childhood years up to age 7, the specter of their actions now tainted my mind.

Vivid flashbacks became an inescapable part of my daily existence, as though my mind was determined to replay the scenes of their violation on an endless loop. Those moments' sights, sounds, and sensations would flood my senses, transporting me back to the very heart of the trauma I endured. It was as if time had folded, blurring the boundaries between past and present, forcing me to relive the horrors I desperately wished to forget. Nightmares would invade my slumber, robbing me of the restorative refuge sleep should have provided. Instead, my subconscious became a theatre for replicating the horrors, a relentless stage where the darkness of their actions took center stage. The haunting dreams served as a cruel reminder that the impact of their transgressions went far beyond waking hours, infiltrating the realm of my unconsciousness and further entangling their presence within the depths of my psyche.

The weight of despair overwhelmed my mind as thoughts of suicide consumed my every waking moment. It felt as though a dark cloud had descended upon my soul, casting a shadow over any glimmer of hope that remained. The sense of purposelessness and hopelessness suffocated any flicker of optimism that dared to emerge. During the darkest moments, I fixated on a seemingly final solution; the river that flowed just a few streets below my house. Its waters called out to me, offering an escape from the pain that enveloped my being. I contemplated jumping into its depths, knowing that I could not swim. The allure of the river's currents promised a relief from the torment, a release from the unbearable weight that burdened my existence.

The lie had lost meaning, and each passing day felt like a relentless battle against the emptiness within. The world around me appeared devoid of color, stripped of joy and purpose. It was thought I had become a mere spectator in my own life, disconnected from the experiences and relationships that once held significance. The future seemed like an impenetrable void devoid of hope and possibility.

Some days I felt rage and anger. Visions of vengeance danced through my mind like a tempest, tempting me with the idea of inflicting upon my abusers the same pain they had inflicted upon me. I found myself entertaining thoughts of retribution, imagining scenarios where they would suffer, where their bodies would bear the physical marks of their heinous acts. Even the notion of resorting to voodoo or other supernatural means to seek justice crossed my mind in moments of darkness. The desire to witness them reduced to utter degradation, scavenging from trash cans because of their actions, briefly flickered like a twisted beacon of satisfaction. However, upon deeper reflection, I realized that such methods would only perpetuate a cycle of insanity; they would not provide the sense of satisfaction that I truly needed.

Then one day, amid the darkness, I realized the urgent need for support and intervention.

I understood that seeking revenge would not bring me the solace or peace I craved. It would not undo the damage or restore the innocence that was taken from me. Inflicting pain upon my abusers would only perpetuate a cycle of violence, perpetuating the darkness that had already consumed so much of my life. I seized self-pity; I seized self-sorrow.

In my relentless pursuit of deliverance, I embarked on a journey to secure job opportunities with the promise of a fresh start. With every application submitted and every interview attended, I hoped to break free from the suffocating grip of my past. However, the cruel irony of my circumstances remained: I still lived within the walls that had witnessed my deepest trauma. Living in the same house where my perpetrators violated me, each day felt like a haunting replay of the horrors I had endured. The room where I had been assaulted became a prison of painful memories, an unyielding reminder of the darkness that had consumed me. The weight of the actions pressed heavily upon me as if the walls were closing in, threatening to suffocate my spirit.

The urgency to escape this suffocating environment grew with each passing day. It became clear that to reclaim my sense of safety and rebuild my shattered self, I had to physically distance myself from the place that held such unbearable memories. The walls that had witnessed my torment needed to be left behind, their echoes fading into the distance as I forged a path toward a new beginning.

Chapter Seven

From Shadows to Light-Breaking the Chains of Childhood Sexual Abuse

A year had passed since I left high school, and amidst my ardent pursuit of independence, I stumbled upon a remarkable opportunity to shape my life's direction. During this pivotal moment of transition, as I yearned to break free from the confines of the house in which I had been raised, that fate intervened and bestowed upon me to work for a market research company. The prospect of embarking on this professional journey filled me with excitement and anticipation.

It represented more than just a job; it signified a stepping stone toward the life I yearned for. The market research industry promised new experiences, learning opportunities, and personal growth that transcended the confines of my previous existence.

I was trained as an interviewer, and the company was run by a well-known and highly respected psychologist who held thought-provoking, albeit controversial, opinions on matters concerning the gender divide. Despite the unique challenges presented by my job, I was grateful for the chance to learn such an impactful figure in the field. While working with him, he had a team of brilliant young psychologists that he hired. One of these bright individuals was still attending university then, but his intelligence and hard work were already evident. We soon became associates; he was transformed into a trusting and enduring friend over time.

On a particular Saturday, I was at the office to drop off some important work materials gathered from the public that day. As I handed them over to my colleague, we immediately clicked, and our friendship started.

As someone who had endured trauma at the hands of men outside my family, trust did not come easily to me. However, he was a different-a kind, empathetic soul who became my haven. Whenever I needed to vent and find solace, he was always there to lend a listening ear. It was comforting to have someone with such a patient demeanor to confide in.

I vividly recall the nights when my world would come crashing down, and I would reach for the phone to call him. He was always there for me, no matter the hour, and I could not be more grateful. On other occasions, he would invite me to his home, where he would whip up some delicious meals and serve them to me at his dining table. Being in a safe space was comforting amongst someone who radiated warmth and exuded trust. My past adolescent experiences left me deeply wounded and damaged. Trusting men, especially those outside my family, such as my dad and uncles, wasn't easy. But being around him gave me hope. He slowly started helping me see that not all men were the same, and for that, I am forever grateful.

I was ecstatic when I received a job from a well-known family planning agency. They wanted me to become a vibrant youth promoter, inspiring and uplifting children in inner-city communities of the bustling metropolis. The opportunity to work with such a prominent organization and positively impact young people's lives was truly exhilarating. This opportunity came to fruition after applying for over a hundred open positions.

Reflecting on my journey, I cannot help but think about how clueless I was when I started working for this organization. The thought of how little I knew compared to how much I have learned over the years still leaves me in awe. Truthfully, I was unaware and unprepared for the emotional challenges ahead of me. Luckily, this organization proactively offered me counseling services right from the onset. Their thoughtful consideration to equip me with mental and emotional tools to handle the weight of the job spoke volumes. Looking back now, I realize that their foresight might have been born from their ability to see through me.

Every day was intense, and I went through the work; I encountered situations that punched through my armor of resilience. Little did I know that the organizational training I received would be the lifeline that kept me afloat amidst the turbulent storms that came my way. I look back now and wholeheartedly credit my transformation to the nurturing offered by the organization that first took a chance on me.

As I reflect on my journey, I recall seeking guidance from a professional counselor who the organization engaged. The counselor was stationed at the main office during my training period, which lasted for one week at the serene North Coast in Ocho Rios. Her warm and encouraging aura changed how I processed and dealt with my thoughts and emotions. Upon returning to Kingston and transitioning into my new role, the counseling sessions continued as she occasionally visited our clinic. I truly appreciated her visits as she was not only my supervisor's supervisor but also someone who brought peace and understanding into my life.

For three glorious years, I was blessed to be a part of an incredible company project that truly inspired me. I was trained to facilitate topics such as Sexuality, Self-Esteem, Self-Confidence, Good Touch and Bad Touch, Relationships, and many other topics related to daily life skills. As I saw the young people in the communities I served to grow and flourish under my guidance, be it at schools, community centers, or churches, I could not help but feel invigorated. It was as though a fire was ignited within me, urging me to give even more of myself. So, I eagerly joined not one but two national youth organizations, where I served as a mentor to some of the most vibrant and dynamic young girls I had ever met. As I watched them learn and grow, my spirit lifted higher. The more I gave of myself, the more I felt this indescribable rush of joy, excitement, and purpose energized me daily. It was a feeling unlike any other I knew I would cherish for the rest of my days.

I had the privilege to be a part of a renowned youth organization committed to advocating for young people's rights. In this setting, I was entrusted with the role of activities coordinator, a demanding position necessitating creativity and resourcefulness. My responsibility was to design and implement programs that raised awareness about our cause and generated the necessary funds to maintain the group's activities. Despite the challenge, the fulfillment I derived from sharpening my skills and contributing to a noble cause was invaluable.

My team and I consistently needed to source funds to support various initiatives, including training sessions, accommodation, transportation, and retreats. Given our organization's extensive presence throughout the Caribbean region, I was afforded the unique chance to interact with an array of extraordinary individuals. These were people driven by a shared passion for effecting meaningful change, and their infectious inspiration left a profound impression. Their unwavering dedication and commitment to our cause undoubtedly brought out the best in me. Their influence had a lasting effect, shaping my triumphs, personal growth, and development in unforgettable ways.

Chapter Eight

Echoes of Discovery-Uncovering My Identity in College

I remember vividly how I felt as my tenure was ending as a Youth Promoter. I knew it was time to make the transition to pursue my career goals as a Guidance Counselor. That is why at age 24, I enrolled in the best teacher's college in the Western Hemisphere to venture on my three-year journey in Education, where I specialized in Guidance and Counseling. It was one of the most exciting moments of my life, and I was determined to make the most of it.

During my first year at this institution, I was fortunate enough to enroll in courses focused on self-actualization. These classes allowed me to dig deep and explore who I was. Through various exercises, assignments, and discussions, I uncovered my likes and dislikes, triggers, and what made me happy or sad. It was a process of self-discovery that was both challenging and rewarding.

As I reflected upon my upbringing and its impact on my state at the time, I was struck by the profound nature of the realization. I discovered so many remarkable qualities in myself-creativity, boldness, self-confidence, and patience-which I had never fully appreciated before. It was an eye-opening experience that helped me to understand the challenges I faced were never my fault and gave me a sense of empowerment as I moved forward.

In my second year, I assumed the role of an exceptional Assistant Unit Leader, and in my third year, I was promoted to Unit Leader. My incredible attention to detail, the relationship-building skills I had acquired, and my meticulous organizational skills undoubtedly contributed to my success in these two roles. I earned my space as a Third-Year Lady Representative by my third year. My natural leadership abilities acquired in my first year and at the beginning of adulthood allowed me to guide and inspire my team toward unity and overall success. My fearlessness and unwavering confidence served as a shining example around me, solidifying my reputation as an exceptional leader with unbreakable self-esteem. That timid melancholic young lady seemed to have vanished in thin air. On the day of graduation, I was incredibly honored to receive a plethora of prestigious awards that recognized my remarkable achievements throughout my academic journey. Among these were the Distinction in Practice of Education award, which lauded my exceptional teaching skills, and a stunning plaque commemorating my outstanding academic record as an Honor Roll student with a 3.5 GPA. Additionally, I was overjoyed to receive the glittering trophy for Best All-Round Teacher, a testament to my hard work, dedication, growth, and unwavering passion for education. I was surprised that I could build myself and conquer my adversities in such a remarkably short time.

Throughout my healing journey, I prioritized engaging in activities that kept me active and involved in my community. Volunteering with organizations like Youth Opportunities Unlimited and the National Youth Service allowed me to give back and help young people become the best version of themselves. I also participated in the Youth Advocacy Movement, Caribbean Chapter, where we educated children and adolescents on sexuality and helped them develop their social skills. Being a part of this movement was an incredibly meaningful and fulfilling experience, and I credit it as one of the most significant parts of my healing journey. These experiences contributed to my overall well-being and helped me develop a greater sense of purpose and meaning.

Through my experiences, I realized the profound impact of staying active and engaged in uplifting activities on my mental wellness. Engaging in these activities was uplifting and a powerful tool that helped me regain calm and balance. These engagements rejuvenated, refreshed, and restorative to my mind and body. They were inspiring, encouraging, and empowering, helping me feel more in control of my life.

I also developed a mindfulness practice that assisted with good mental health. Practicing meditation, reflection, and gratitude regularly contributed to my sense of well-being. I also engaged in activities such as relaxation, exercise, and journaling, which served as opportunities for introspection and growth.

Throughout my recovery, I prioritized engaging

in activities that kept me active and involved in my community. Volunteering with organizations like Youth Opportunities Unlimited and the National Youth Service allowed me to give back and help young people become the best version of themselves. I also participated in the Youth Advocacy Movement, Caribbean Chapter, where we educated children and adolescents on sexuality and helped them develop their social skills. Being a part of this movement was an incredibly meaningful and fulfilling experience, and I credit it as one of the most significant parts of my healing journey. These experiences contributed to my overall well-being and helped me develop a greater sense of purpose and meaning.

Chapter Nine

Prevalence and Stats on Child Abuse

The National Center for Victims of Crime website states that the extent of child sexual abuse remains difficult to ascertain due to its largely unreported nature. Shockingly, the number of cases of such abuse is far greater than those officially documented by authorities, underscoring the magnitude of the problem. The profound silence often accompanies such abuse, enveloping the victim in a cloak of shame, terror, and despair. Many children suffer silently, overwhelmed by confusion, helplessness, and betrayal. The prevalence of this wicked act is all too pervasive and insidious, bringing incalculable pain and trauma to its victims.

The consequences of such abuse are profound, inflicting serious damage on the victim's sense of self-worth, confidence, and trust in others. The persistent harm such abuse causes may manifest for years, or even decades following the occurrence, influencing the victim's emotional and psychological well-being in ways that may reverberate throughout their lifetime. The true extent of this atrocity must be recognized and addressed, with a concerted effort to raise public awareness and encourage victims to come forward and seek help. Only by understanding the reality of this issue and supporting those who suffer may we hope to reduce the terrible burden on society.

According to studies conducted by David Finkelhor, the Director of the Crimes Against Children Research Center, the prevalence of child abuse is deeply disturbing. Astonishingly, one in five girls and one in 20 boys are victims of this abuse, a staggering statistic that is both disheartening and alarming. Adding to this alarming reality is that sexual victimization often begins at a young age, with children between the ages of 7 and 13 being the most vulnerable.

During their lifetime, a significant portion of U.S. children aged 14 to 17, approximately 28%, have experienced sexual victimization at some point in their lives, leaving a lasting impact that may take years to recover from fully.

It is important to note that the prevalence of childhood sexual abuse is not limited to these age groups. In fact, according to Finkelhor's research, self-reported studies have shown that a significant number of adult females, around 20%, and 5-10% of adult males recall experiencing sexual abuse or assault as children.

The issue of child sexual abuse and solutions extends far beyond mere statistics, touching the very core of society and challenging us to be vigilant and proactive in protecting the most vulnerable among us. It is crucial to raise awareness and encourage an open dialogue around sexual abuse, breaking down societal taboos that too often prevent victims from coming forward and receiving the help they need.

The National Institute of Justice released a report in 2003 which highlights the harrowing statistics surrounding sexual assault among adolescents. The report reveals that perpetrators abused a staggering 75% of adolescent victims of sexual assault that they knew personally (page 5). This alarming reality highlights the importance of constant vigilance and protective measures for parents and caregivers regarding adolescents' safety and well-being. It is crucial to equip children with knowledge and strategies to recognize and avoid potentially dangerous situations while keeping an open communication line to facilitate healing and recovery should they fall victim to such trauma.

It is incredibly important for parents and caregivers to stay vigilant when monitoring changes in their children's behavior. Sometimes, it can be easy to get caught up in the hustle and bustle of daily life and forget to prioritize our little ones. One of the keys to staying on top of things is to make a conscious effort to remain engaged in our children's lives. This could mean setting aside time for conversations, participating in activities, or simply being present when they need our support.

According to a report from the Bureau of Justice, children who are not living with both of their parents or those living in homes experiencing domestic violence or divorce face a greater risk of being subjected to sexual abuse. This report highlights the alarming reality of the potential correlation between experiencing instability in the home environment and increased susceptibility to sexual abuse. The findings suggest that children in these vulnerable living situations are more prone to victimization, which calls for greater support and intervention services for families and children who may be at risk. These findings emphasize the importance of awareness and education on the dangers of sexual abuse and the need for a safe and stable living environment for children.

Stopping abuse, especially child abuse, is a complex issue that requires the involvement of various stakeholders, such as parents, educators, mental health professionals, and law enforcement officials. To effectively combat abuse, we must all be united and committed to creating a safer, more transparent world by encouraging open conversations about it. By joining forces and taking determined steps, we can work towards a world where abuse is no longer tolerated, and our children can grow up in a safe and nurturing environment. This involves fostering an environment that values transparency, accountability, and a zero-tolerance approach toward abuse. Achieving this goal requires all hands on deck, working together to create a safer future for our children.

Chapter Ten

Grooming the Innocent

Child sexual abuse constitutes a horrendous crime, with victims often enduring long-term, harmful effects that can severely impact their mental health, interpersonal relationships, and overall well-being. A common strategy employed by abusers to gain access to children is through a technique known as grooming.

Grooming is a complex, calculated process, executed over time, where the abuser strategically engages in specific behaviors to establish a relationship with the child. The grooming aims to form an emotional dependency between the child and the abuser, effectively shifting the power balance in the latter's favor. This process involves earning the child's trust, normalizing inappropriate conduct, and fostering emotional bonds.

The abuser may extend these manipulative relationships to the child's family, peers, and entire communities. In doing so, they create avenues of access to the child and manage to exert control over them without arousing suspicion from their surroundings. These manipulative behaviors can often be subtle, going unnoticed by others. They can be challenging to identify, hence the need to gain a greater understanding of grooming and safeguarding children against such forms of abuse.Bottom of Form

Unfortunately,Building trust is one of the primary tactics they use during this process. This may involve offering gifts, kind gestures, or attention to the child to win their favor and create a sense of attachment. Perpetrators may also pose as mentors, teachers, or authority figures in the child's life, using their position of authority to gain the child's trust and admiration. Along with these more overt tactics, perpetrators may also use subtle manipulation strategies to create a sense of trust with the child. They offer words of flattery, compliments, or even seemingly innocuous questions and conversation topics to make the child feel heard and valued. This process may be gradual and intentional, with the perpetrator working to make the child feel comfortable in their presence and trust them more and more over time.

While building trust is ongoing, culprits may also work to test the waters with the child, experimenting with more risky behavior or discussions to gauge the child's level of comfort and interest. For example, they may introduce sexual topics or imagery into conversations or show inappropriate child materials to test their reaction and desire for further interactions. Ultimately, the process helps perpetrators establish initial connections with children and gradually escalate their abuse without causing alarm or suspicion. They may seek to normalize the behavior by presenting it as acceptable or commonplace.

During the 'testing the water' phase, the perpetrator looks for signs that the child may be more receptive to their advances. If the child expresses curiosity or interest in the sexual content and demonstrates a lack of resistance, or revulsion, the perpetrator may feel emboldened to continue their grooming tactics. At this point, they may escalate the sexual activity or conversation and continue normalizing it as a part of their relationship with the child.

It is important to note that this process of testing the waters is often carefully calculated and paced by the abuser and may occur over an extended period. By gradually escalating the sexual content or behavior, they can avoid tipping off the child or anyone else to their intentions while increasing their hold over the child and exerting greater control in the relationship.

Another commonly used tactic used by perpetrators during grooming is isolation. This involves various methods of separating the child from their social supports, including their peers and family. The perpetrator may discourage the child from participating in activities with their peers and family. They may discourage the child from participating in activities with their friends, making them feel dependent on the culprit for companionship and emotional support. They may also work to decrease the child's contact with their family or caregivers, creating an environment in which the perpetrator has greater control over the child's interactions and experiences. Perpetrators may also engage in activities with the child only between them, further isolating the child from other relationships and forcing their dependence on them. These activities may be presented as special treats or privileges, further cementing the child's attachment and making it more difficult for them to resist their advances. By isolating the child from social support in these ways, violators can increase their power and control over the child, making it easier for them to manipulate and exploit the child without fear of detection. In many cases, the isolation tactics used are both subtle and insidious, making them difficult to recognize and respond to before significant harm has been done.

Violators of sexual abuse may also use a tactic called desensitization as a part of their grooming process. Desensitization involves slowly and gradually introducing the child to unwanted touch and sexual behavior to make them more comfortable with these actions over time. The perpetrators may begin by engaging in innocuous behaviors, such as hugging or tickling, before gradually escalating to more intrusive or inappropriate behaviors. Victimizers may use various methods to desensitize children, such as undressing in front of them or touching their private areas. They may also engage in simulated sex acts, using suggestive actions or language to normalize the behavior and make the child more accepting. These behaviors may be presented as games or playful activities or used to reward the child's compliance or corporation.

Desensitization tactics are particularly insidious, as they can desensitize children to behaviors that they normally find uncomfortable or inappropriate. Over time, the child may accept these behaviors as normal or enjoy them, making it easier for the perpetrator to continue escalating the abuse. Desensitization risks the child losing their sense of physical and emotional boundaries, leading to difficulties in recognizing and stopping abusive behavior in the future.

Child molesters may use fear and intimidation tactics to keep their victims quiet. This could involve threats to the child or their family or efforts to blackmail and coerce them into remaining silent about the abuse they have suffered or witnessed. Such tactics can be especially traumatic and damaging to young and vulnerable individuals, as they may feel trapped, helpless, and unsure of where to turn for help or support. As a society, we must recognize and address these threats and work to provide safe and supportive environments where children can speak out and seek justice without fear of reprisals or retribution.

Abusers may also utilize a form of psychological manipulation which can take several forms. One such form is emotional manipulation, where the perpetrator may create a sense of guilt or obligation for the child. This can be achieved in various ways, such as by making the child feel responsible for the abuse or convincing them that they must keep it a secret. Furthermore, psychological coercion may also be used, which can involve forcing the child to comply with the abuser's wishes using threats or force. Also, positive reinforcement may be utilized, wherein they may offer rewards or praise to the child in exchange for their corporation or silence about the abuse. All these forms of manipulation can be extremely damaging and result in long-lasting psychological trauma and emotional harm.

Perpetrators of grooming behavior are usually adept at hiding their intentions and maneuvers at establishing trust and communication in secluded circumstances. They use these environments to gain access and control over their victims, rendering them powerless to resist the offender's advances. It is also common for violators to target individuals with existing vulnerabilities or unstable family dynamics, exploiting their emotional state to gain access to the victim.

The effects of grooming behavior on children are devastating. Once the abuser has gained the child's trust, it becomes increasingly challenging for the child to recognize the predatory behavior. Moreover, children may feel trapped and hesitant to tell anyone about the abuse due to the manipulated relationship. This can result in destructive effects on their mental health, like PTSD, anxiety, and depression, all of which can continue to affect them throughout adulthood.

Chapter Eleven

Symptoms and Signs of Childhood Sexual Abuse

It is heartbreaking to know that children who experience this kind of trauma can suffer from a range of physical, emotional, and behavioral symptoms that can impact their lives.

According to the Bureau of Justice Statistics, children who are victims of prolonged sexual abuse are particularly vulnerable to negative psychological effects. This can include low self-esteem, a feeling of worthlessness, and mistrust and withdrawal from adult figures they may have once looked to for safety and support. Sadly, for some victims, the pain and trauma of sexual abuse can become so overwhelming that they may experience suicidal thoughts or engage in self-harm to cope. These symptoms can be difficult to manage and make daily life difficult for those affected.

According to Rape Abuse Incest National Network (RAINN), see below the behavioral, physical, and emotional indicators of childhood sexual abuse.

BEHAVIORAL SIGNS

1. Excessive talking about or knowledge of sexual topics

Excessive talking about or knowledge of sexual topics in a child could be a red flag that something is amiss. This behavior could indicate exposure to inappropriate materials like pornography or even signify sexual abuse. Children who have experienced sexual abuse may have a distorted sense of appropriate and normal sexual behavior and may exhibit behaviors that are highly sexualized or even for their age. By engaging in conversations about sexual topics that are confusing or inappropriate for their age, these children could knowingly disclose that something is wrong. As such, it is important to take this behavior seriously and investigate further to determine the root cause and take appropriate steps to protect the child's well-being.

2. Keeping secrets and not talking as much as before

This could be indicative of emotional distress, fear, or even abuse. Sometimes children experiencing sexual abuse may keep secrets to avoid criticism or punishment. They often fear for their safety. If a child suddenly becomes less talkative or withdraws from activities previously enjoyed, it may be a sign that something is wrong. It is imperative to create a safe environment where children feel comfortable sharing their thoughts and feelings and to be on the lookout for changes in behavior that signal that they may need additional support or intervention.

3. Refuses to be left alone with certain people or is afraid to be away from the primary caregiver

When innocent children become victims of unfathomable trauma inflicted upon them through sexual abuse, one of the distressing ways in which this trauma can manifest is through a notable transformation in behavior. Specifically, these courageous young souls may exhibit an unwelcome shift in their inclination, now displaying a newfound aversion to finding themselves in isolated settings with specific individuals. This hesitance, coupled with a heightened fear of separation from their primary caregiver, lays the deep-seated wounds engrained in them by their stressful experience of sexual abuse. They will sometimes say things such as 'I don't want to go back to Grandma's house,' or they will express distress in having a specific person over to babysit.

4. **Regressive behaviors or resuming behaviors they had outgrown**

When children undergo the traumatic experience of sexual abuse, its profound impact on their emotional and psychological well-being can manifest in various ways. One such manifestation is the emergence of regressive behaviors, which revert to previously outgrown behavior patterns as a coping mechanism. These regressive behaviors remind them of their vulnerability and their distress. Examples of such regressive behaviors include bedwetting and thumb sucking, which were once behaviors typically associated with earlier stages of development. The resumption of these behaviors can be seen as a subconscious attempt to find comfort and security when they feel safer and more protected. The return to these childhood behaviors represents a poignant expression of their inner turmoil and desperate need for reassurance and care. Recognizing and understanding these behaviors is crucial for caregivers and professionals to provide the necessary support and therapeutic interventions to help them navigate the path toward healing and recovery.

5. Sexual behavior that is inappropriate for the child's age

One distressing way this trauma can manifest is by displaying inappropriate sexual behavior beyond what is developmentally appropriate for their age. These children, who should be immersed in the innocent joys of childhood, may exhibit a range of deeply troubling behaviors. They may engage in sexual acts, use sexualized language or gestures, or demonstrate excessive preoccupation with sexual themes. These behaviors are stark reminders of the unimaginable violation they have endured and the profound disruption inflicted upon their healthy sexual development.

Such inappropriate sexual behaviors in abused children serve as a distressing reflection of the trauma they have experienced. They are attempting to navigate and make sense of their traumatic experiences in a deeply confusing and troubling way for themselves and those around them. Understanding and addressing these behaviors require a compassionate and comprehensive approach involving skilled professionals specializing in trauma-informed care.

6. Overly compliant behavior

One unusual behavior that may emerge is excessive and exaggerated compliance in their interactions and relationships. These overly compliant behaviors are a coping mechanism rooted in fear, confusion, and a desperate desire to please others. This behavior can be characterized by an exaggerated eagerness to please authority figures, a reluctance to express personal preferences or boundaries, and an excessive need for external validation and approval. This behavior is a reflection they endured, as they may internalize the deep-seated belief that compliance will protect them from further harm or rejection. They may suppress their needs, desires, and emotions to maintain control or avoid potential retribution.

Recognizing and understanding this over-compliant behavior is crucial for caregivers, educators, and professionals involved in the child's support system. It is essential to create a safe and nurturing environment that encourages the child's autonomy, fosters healthy assertiveness, and promotes the development of personal boundaries. By providing therapeutic interventions, empathy, and consistent care, we can help these brave young individuals restore their sense of self-worth and rebuild their ability to navigate relationships in a healthy and balanced manner.

7. Trying to avoid removing clothing when it is time for bathing or changing

Among the heartbreaking effects of sexual abuse on younger children, one distressing behavior that may emerge is their resistance to removing clothing during routine activities such as bathing or changing. These innocent souls, who should feel secure and protected, may exhibit signs of discomfort, fear, or distress when faced with the need to undress. For these children, undressing can trigger traumatic memories, evoke feelings of vulnerability, or remind them of the violation they endured. Their resistance to removing clothing during these essential activities is an expression of pain, confusion, and attempts to safeguard themselves from further harm.

Caregivers, professionals, and support systems must approach this behavior with sensitivity, empathy, and understanding. By creating a safe and nurturing environment that respects their boundaries, allows them to express their feelings, and provides reassurance, we can rebuild their trust and help them regain a sense of safety and control over their bodies.

8. Spending an unusual amount of time alone

One noticeable behavioral response in children who experience sexual abuse is their tendency to spend an unusual and prolonged time in solitude. They may retreat from social interactions and seek solace in their own company. The increased preference for solitude can stem from various underlying factors. It may serve as a coping mechanism, allowing the child to create a sense of control and safety by avoiding potential triggers or harmful situations. It can also be an attempt to withdraw from overwhelming emotions, a way to process the traumatic experiences they have endured. This can also manifest in their struggle with trust and forming connections with others. The deep-seated fear of vulnerability and the lingering effects of abuse may hinder their ability to engage in meaningful social interactions or seek support from others.

PHYSICAL SIGNS

1. Sexually transmitted infection

When children are subjected to the horrifying ordeal of sexual abuse, one unfortunate consequence that may manifest is the presence of signs indicating a sexually transmitted infection (STI). Sexual abuse can involve forced sexual contact, which puts the child at risk of contracting infections transmitted through sexual activity. Common STIs in abused children can include genital itching, sores, rashes, discharge, pain or discomfort during urination, or unusual changes in the genital appearance. These distressing indications are tangible reminders of the violation they have endured and the potential health consequences they now face.

Caregivers, medical professionals, and support systems must take prompt action to ensure proper medical evaluation, diagnosis, and treatment for any suspected STIs. This involves providing a safe and confidential space for the child to disclose their experiences, seek appropriate medical attention, and provide necessary support through the healing process.

2. Signs of trauma on the genital area

When children suffer the unspeakable horrors of sexual abuse, the physical consequences can be particularly devastating, manifesting in various visible signs of trauma on their genital area. These distressing indicators, including unexplained bleeding, bruising, or the discovery of blood on their sheets, underwear, or clothing, stand as undeniable evidence of the violation and brutality they have endured. These signs of trauma are a stark reminder of the physical harm inflicted upon their bodies, highlighting the profound violation of their boundaries and the lasting impact of the abuse. The presence of unexplained bleeding or bruising on the genital area unveils the depth of the trauma experienced by the victims.

Urgent medical attention is essential to document the physical evidence, assess the extent of the trauma, and provide appropriate medical care.

EMOTIONAL SIGNS

1. Change in Eating Habits.

When a child becomes a victim of sexual abuse, the profound impact of this traumatic experience may exhibit alterations in their relationship with food and eating habits. The effects may vary as some children experience a loss of appetite, leading to a significant decrease in food intake and weight loss. In contrast, others may turn to food as a coping mechanism, resulting in excessive eating and weight gain. The changes in eating behaviors reflect the complex interplay between the psychological responses to the trauma they have endured. The shift in eating habits is a visible sign of the distress and turmoil within these young individuals. It can manifest their attempt to gain control in a world where they have been violated and stripped of their innocence. Food becomes entangled with their emotions, coping with overwhelming fear, shame, or powerlessness.

Understanding that the change in eating habits is not merely a matter of appetite but a reflection of the deep-rooted trauma they have experienced is fundamental in providing the compassionate care victims deserve. With a comprehensive approach, we can empower them to restore their physical and emotional well-being, helping them reclaim their sense of agency and regain trust in their bodies.

2. Change in mood or personality.

The emotional and psychological toll of childhood sexual abuse can lead to noticeable changes in mood or personality. These resilient young souls, who should be basking in the joys of childhood, may exhibit significant shifts towards either extreme aggression or withdrawal and silence. Some children may externalize their pain and confusion through aggressive behavior, displaying heightened anger, irritability, and even violence toward others. This aggression can serve as a defense mechanism, an outlet for the intense emotions they grapple with, or an attempt to control a chaotic and unsafe world.

On the other hand, some children may internalize their pain, retreating into a state of profound silence and withdrawal. They may become unusually quiet, reserved, or detached from social interactions. This withdrawal can be a protective response, a means of self-preservation, or an effort to conceal their vulnerability and fear. Victims are grappling with complex emotions, struggling to make sense of the violation they have endured, and searching for ways to navigate their shattered sense of safety and trust, exhibited through aggression or silence.

3. Decrease in confidence or self-image.

The trauma of sexual can deeply impact a child's perception of themselves and their place in the world. They may internalize feelings of shame, guilt, and worthlessness, believing that they are somehow responsible for the abuse they endured. This distorted self-perception can lead to a sharp decline in confidence, causing them to doubt their abilities, talents, and personal worth. They may suffer from profoundly erasing their self-esteem and overall sense of self-worth. The violation of their boundaries and the breach of trust they experienced can shatter their sense of safety and security. This can further contribute to a negative self-image as they struggle to regain control and navigate the overwhelming emotions associated with their traumatic experience.

4. Excessive worry or fearfulness.

Childhood sexual abuse can deeply shake a child's sense of safety and trust in the world around them. They may develop a pervasive sense of unease and apprehension, fearing potential threats and dangers even in seemingly innocuous situations. This excessive worry and fearfulness can manifest as heightened vigilance, constant anticipation of harm, and an inability to relax or feel at ease. The roots of this behavior lie in the traumatic experiences they have endured. Sexual abuse inflicts overpowering emotional wounds, leaving them vulnerable and hyperaware of potential dangers. Fearfulness and excessive worry serve as defense mechanisms to stay on guard and protect themselves from further harm. These young individuals, who should be free to explore the world with a sense of security, may instead find themselves trapped in a web of overwhelming anxiety and fear.

5. Increase in unexplained health problems such as stomach aches and headaches.

One distressing consequence that may arise with childhood sexual abuse is unexplained health problems, specifically ailments such as stomach aches and headaches. The correlation between the trauma inflicted by the activities and the emergence of unexplained health problems is complex and multifaceted. The psychological distress endured by these vulnerable children can result in bodily ways, where the engrained emotional turmoil they experienced is translated into physical discomfort and pain. The profound violation of their bodies, coupled with the intense emotional upheaval, can disrupt the delicate balance of their nervous system, triggering a cascade of physiological responses that manifest as persistent stomach aches and headaches.

6. **Loss or decreased interest in school, activities, and friends.**

The impact of sexual abuse on a child's enthusiasm for school, activities, and social connections is far-reaching. Their emotional and psychological trauma can disrupt their ability to focus, concentrate, and participate actively in educational settings. The once vibrant curiosity and eagerness to learn may dwindle, replaced by detachment, disinterest, or even avoidance of school-related activities. The effects of sexual abuse can seep into a child's engagement in extracurricular activities and hobbies that once brought them joy. Their trauma may overshadow their ability to derive pleasure or fulfillment from these pursuits. They may withdraw from previously enjoyed activities, lose motivation to participate, or struggle to find solace and connection in the company of their peers.

The impact on their friendships is equally significant. Sexual abuse can fracture their trust in others, making it difficult for them to form and maintain meaningful relationships. The once vibrant and flourishing connections with friends may wane as the child is consumed with a sense of vulnerability, fear, or a distorted self-perception resulting from the abuse. They may isolate themselves, have trouble trusting others, or withdraw from social interactions.

7. Nightmares or fear of being alone at night.

When darkness falls and the night envelops the world, children who have endured the indescribable trauma of sexual abuse may find themselves consumed with ongoing challenges. Within the nighttime realm, they may encounter distressing nightmares that haunt their dreams or experience an overpowering fear of solitude that controls their nighttime hours. In addition to the turmoil of nightmares, a deep-seated fear of being alone at night may take hold. The encompassing darkness may starkly remind them of the violation inflicted upon them, amplifying their vulnerability and triggering intense anxiety. The solitude of the night may feel suffocating as they long for the presence and reassurance of a trusted caregiver or loved one to provide a shield against the perceived threats that lurk in the shadows.

The nocturnal struggles, whether in the form of distressing nightmares or a fear of isolation, remind us of the enduring impact of sexual abuse on a child's sense of safety and tranquility. Their trauma casts a long and haunting shadow, infiltrating their dreams' sanctuary and instilling a deep-seated unease even in moments of supposed rest.

8. Self-harming behaviors.

Self-harming behaviors are sometimes the result of the devastating effects of sexual abuse in children. They may exhibit these behaviors in response to their pain and anguish to cope and express their distress. These self-destructive actions manifest in various forms from the topsy-turvy in their heads and the desperate need to find an outlet for their overwhelming emotions.

Self-harming behaviors can manifest in different ways, such as cutting, burning, scratching, hitting oneself, or engaging in risky behaviors that jeopardize their physical well-being. These actions are not attention-seeking or manipulative but rather a desperate attempt to cope with the pain they carry within. The complex interplay between the traumatic experience and sexual abuse and self-harming is engrained in the psychological and emotional aftermath of the abuse victims endured.

Chapter Twelve

Coping with Child Sexual Abuse

The revelation that one's child has been subjected to the unspeakable trauma of sexual abuse is an overwhelmingly distressing and formidable experience for any parent. Coping with such a revelation requires immense strength and support.

SEEK PROFESSIONAL HELP

In the face of the profound challenges brought about by the discovery of your child's experience with sexual abuse, it is crucial to take a proactive approach and seek professional support from a highly trained therapist or counselor who specializes in trauma and sexual abuse. These dedicated professionals possess a wealth of knowledge, skills, and experience that essentially provide invaluable support and guidance to both you as a parent and your child. They can help process emotions, provide coping strategies, and navigate the complex healing process.

EDUCATION

Empowering yourself with knowledge is vital in supporting your child's healing journey and effectively addressing the impact of sexual abuse. Take the time and effort to educate yourself about the intricate and far-reaching effects of sexual abuse, the specific ways it impacts children, and the complex healing and recovery process. By immersing yourself in learning, you gain a deeper understanding of the dynamics of abuse and its consequences. Educating yourself about the emotional, phycological, and physical effects your child may experience enables you to respond with empathy, sensitivity, and informed decision-making.

Expand your knowledge of the common behavioral, emotional, and cognitive manifestations of abuse in children. Understand their potential relationship challenges, academic performance, self-esteem, and overall well-being. Recognize that the healing process is unique to everyone, and familiarize yourself with evidence-based therapeutic interventions, coping strategies, and support resources available.

Acquiring knowledge about the legal and medical aspects of addressing sexual abuse is equally important. Be vigilant of the reporting and legal procedures associated, such as understanding mandatory reporting laws and cooperating with law enforcement or child protective services. Become educated on the available medical examinations and treatments that may be necessary and the importance of maintaining the privacy and confidentiality of your child's medical records. By becoming well-informed, you can advocate more effectively for your child's needs and navigate the various systems involved in their recovery process. Knowledge equips you to communicate with professionals, ask the correct questions, and make informed decisions in the child's best interest.

ENCOURAGE OPEN COMMUNICATION

One crucial aspect of supporting a child who has experienced sexual abuse is fostering an environment of open communication. It involves creating a safe, non-judgmental space where the child feels comfortable sharing their feelings, fears, and experiences. By actively encouraging and facilitating open dialogue, we can empower the child to express themselves and provide them with the support they need to heal. Trust must be established so the child feels safe sharing their emotions. This involves listening to their concerns, validating their feelings, and assuring them that their experiences are taken seriously. Demonstrating empathy can create an atmosphere where the child feels heard, acknowledged, and safe from criticism and judgment.

It is also important to be patient and allow the child to express themselves at their own pace. Do not rush or pressure them to disclose information before they are ready. Let them feel comfortable expressing themselves by providing reassurance that their feelings and experiences are valid. Please encourage them to share as little or as much as they feel comfortable with, making them feel like they are in control of their narrative. Additionally, the child should not be blamed or shamed. Provide support by telling the child they are not at fault and that you believe their story. The child will then be encouraged to speak openly. Always maintain eye contact, nod, and give affirming gestures to show that you are fully present and attentive.

By fostering open communication, we create

a foundation of trust and safety for the child. This will enable them to navigate their healing process, knowing they have a reliable and supportive person to turn to. By encouraging self-expression and actively listening, we show our commitment to their well-being and provide them with the vital emotional support they need on their journey to recovery.

VALIDATE EMOTIONS

Validating the emotions that come with childhood sexual abuse and rape is essential, as it acknowledges the complex and intense nature of the trauma they have endured. Understanding that sadness, confusion, anger, shame, and guilt are all natural and valid responses to the situation. Validating emotions can foster a supportive environment for healing. When a child's emotions are validated, we demonstrate a willingness to listen and accept their feelings without judgment. We reassure them that their reactions are normal. Validating their emotions encourages them to express themselves freely, promoting their emotional health and aiding in the process of the trauma they have experienced.

It is natural and normal for parents to experience

a range of conflicting emotions, such as anger towards the perpetrator, guilt for not being able to protect their child, shame about the incident, sadness for the loss of innocence, and confusion about navigating the situation. Parents should acknowledge these emotions because by doing so, they acknowledge the profound impact that sexual abuse has on the entire family. Through emotional validation, we affirm the child's and parent's worthiness in recognizing and accepting their emotions. This validation is a powerful tool in healing, fostering a sense of empowerment.

PRIORITIZE SELF-CARE

Taking care of yourself physically and emotionally is vital in maintaining strength throughout this stressful process. By engaging in activities that promote relaxation, self-reflection, and rejuvenation, your energy can be replenished and your energy enhanced for you to be present for your child.

Always set aside time for self-care practices, including exercise, a balanced diet, and getting restful sleep. Doing this can enhance your overall vitality and help you better cope with the emotional demands of the situation. Equally important is addressing your emotional needs. Seek out supportive outlets to process and share your own emotions and experiences. Trusted friends, understanding family members, or support groups can provide a supportive and compassionate space to express your feelings, concerns, and uncertainties. Sharing your thoughts and emotions with others who can empathize and offer support can alleviate the weight of the problem you carry and foster a sense of camaraderie.

Practice mindfulness or meditation to cultivate calm and inner clarity. Taking time for hobbies or engaging in nature can serve as outlets for self-expression and a means to recharge the spirit. Set aside time for introspection and practice activities such as journaling or seeking therapy or counseling. By caring for your well-being, you are better equipped to provide the necessary support and strength your child needs. Self-care allows you to approach the situation with a clearer mind and a more grounded presence and enhances emotional resilience.

ENGAGE IN FAMILY THERAPY

Embrace the healing of family therapy as a valuable resource for addressing the effects of sexual abuse within the entire family unit. Engaging in family therapy creates an opportunity to collectively navigate the impact of the abuse on family dynamics and start a healing journey. Family therapy provides a safe and supportive space for open conversations and understanding. It enables each family member to express their emotions, concerns, and thoughts about sexual abuse. Through guided discussions and therapeutic interventions, family therapy can help untangle the complexities of the abuse's impact on family relationships, communication patterns, and functioning.

In family therapy, a skilled counselor or therapist with experience in sexual abuse and trauma can facilitate communication and guide the family toward healthy coping mechanisms and effective problem-solving strategies. They can help family members develop a more in-depth comprehension of the emotional needs of the survivor, foster empathy, and strengthen bonds of love and support within the family. Family therapy is a collaborative process, and it is important to prioritize the needs and comfort of the survivor through the therapeutic journey. When a family engages in family therapy, they embark on a transformative journey to heal wounds, cultivate an environment of love, strengthen relationships, and enable resilience for the entire family.

PRACTICE SELF COMPASSION

When coping with your child's sexual abuse,

cultivate self-compassion as an essential part of the healing journey. Acknowledge how strenuous and emotionally challenging the healing process can be, and grant yourself the kindness and patience you deserve. Recognize that healing takes time, and that is no specific time for recovery. Allow the self to experience the process and embrace emotions such as guilt, sadness, anger, and grief, all without judgment or self-blame. Accept the truth that it is natural to feel overwhelmed and that seeking professional help is a brave step toward healing. Engage in self-care activities that nurture your physical, emotional, and mental well-being. Lean on your support network during this challenging time. Share your feelings and experiences with trusted friends, family members, or support groups who can provide a listening ear, empathy, and practical assistance.

Practice self-compassion by challenging any self-critical thoughts that may surface. Remind yourself that you are doing your best, that it is a very difficult situation, and that seeking help is a sign of your strength, not weakness. Embrace the resilience and courage you demonstrate on this journey. It will never be easy, but applying some strategies will allow you to cope as best as possible.

Chapter Thirteen

Reducing the Risk of Childhood Sexual Abuse

ESTABLISH BOUNDARIES

To prioritize the safety and well-being of your child, it is crucial to establish a comprehensive and proactive approach, including setting clear boundaries and implementing necessary precautions. Start by defining and communicating clear boundaries with your child. Encourage open and honest communication where they feel comfortable sharing any concerns or discomfort they may experience, no matter what it is.

At home, take steps to create a safe and secure environment. Install a home security system, having proper supervision. Implement age-appropriate privacy measures such as locking doors or using child safety devices. In educational settings, collaborate with school administrators, teachers, and counselors, to ensure your child's safety. Encourage staff members who can provide support to implement measures such as increased supervision, buddy systems, or special accommodations to promote your child's well-being and security, and the other children in the school as well. In social spaces, be mindful of who your child interacts with and the environments they are exposed to. Establish guidelines for social activities, online interactions, and outings. Stay informed about your child's social circle and monitor their online presence to ensure their safety and protect them from potential harm. Regularly reassess and adapt safety measures as needed.

Teach your child about personal boundaries and the concept of private parts. Inform them that certain body parts are private and should not be touched by others unless it is for medical or hygiene purposes, and a trusted adult must be present. Educate your child that no one can touch them on any body part or make them feel uncomfortable. No one should tickle them, rub their hair, etc.; children should know their bodies belong to them. Additionally, remind your child that they do not have the right to touch someone else, especially if they do not want to be touched.

TEACH YOUR CHILD HOW TO TALK ABOUT THEIR BODIES

Starting early, introduce your child to the appropriate names for their body parts, using language suitable for their age. Treat discussions about body parts as you would any other topic or conversation, helping your child recognize that it is perfectly acceptable to talk about their bodies. Also, create an environment where your child can ask questions about their bodies. Encourage curiosity and provide honest, age-appropriate information in response to their inquiries. By fostering an atmosphere of open communication, you allow your child to feel comfortable approaching you whenever they have questions or need clarification.

Establishing an open-door policy ensures your child understands they can always turn to you for guidance and support. Let them know that you are available to listen to their concerns without judgment and that you are there to provide accurate information and assistance. By maintaining this approachable and supportive stance, you reinforce that discussing their bodies and seeking understanding is normal and encouraged. Following these strategies lays the groundwork for healthy communication about their bodies, helping your child develop a strong sense of awareness, confidence, and the ability to speak openly about their experiences.

CHOOSE CAREGIVERS CAREFULLY

When entrusting your child's care to others, it is critical to exercise diligence and caution. This does not guarantee mistreatment, but it will surely minimize the risks. Here are some steps to carefully choose caregivers:

1. Before selecting a caregiver, investigate their background, qualifications, and reputation. Gather information via recommendations and online reviews (if any), and get references.

2. Investigate credentials and certification by verifying the caregiver's certifications and qualifications. Additionally, ensure that they have undergone appropriate screenings and background checks.

3. Conduct in-person interviews with potential caregivers. Uncover their experience working with children, how they discipline, their knowledge of child safety protocols, and how they handle emergencies.

4. Never ignore your instincts. If you feel it,

then it is probably so. If something feels off or raises a red flag, it is important to take those feelings seriously.

5. If considering a new school or activity, visit the facility in person to assess safety measures, cleanliness, and the environment. Observe how staff members interact with the children present and ask about their policies and procedures for child protection.

6. Communicate openly and honestly with potential caregivers about expectations, concerns, and any specific needs your child may have. Clear communication is vital to ensure everyone agrees on the same page regarding care for your child.

7. Regularly assess the caregiver and monitor your child's well-being and comfort level in their care. Encourage your child always to express their feelings about the caregiver and inform you if they feel uncomfortable about anything.

DISCUSS THE MEDIA

Here are examples of questions you can ask your child to initiate a conversation about the media's coverage of incidents of sexual violence:

1. Do you think it is important for the media to cover these incidents? Why or why not?

2. Have you ever observed any incidents or situations of sexual violence on TV shows, social media, or the movies?

3. What actions do you think the media can take to responsibly report incidents of sexual violence without causing any harm?

4. How do you feel when you hear stories about sexual violence in the media?

5. If you happened to witness or hear of someone being sexually abused, what would you have done? Who would you tell? Where would you go for help?

Practice active listening when having these conversations. It is essential to validate their feelings and opinions. Be prepared to provide accurate information, reinforce the importance of consent and boundaries, and emphasize supporting survivors and seeking help.

BE AVAILABLE

Being available and attentive to your child's needs is crucial in creating a supportive environment for open communication. Dedicate specific times or create routines where you can spend quality time with your child. This could be designated family time, bedtime, or meal time, where you give your child undivided attention, allowing them to feel valued and heard. Inform your child that they can approach you at a time without fear if they have questions or if someone makes them feel uncomfortable. Always reinforce your willingness to listen and help. Practice active listening when your child comes to you with questions or concerns. Listen with your entire being. Remain eye contact and ask open-ended follow-up questions to show that you are completely interested in what they are saying and for clarification to ensure that you understand the meaning of what they are trying to convey.

If you do not have all the answers during the conversation, be honest with your child and offer to seek out additional information or resources together. This teaches them the importance of ongoing learning and seeking guidance when necessary. The goal is to establish a strong foundation of open communication and trust with your child. Be available and responsive, and create a safe space so your child will feel comfortable approaching you with questions, concerns, or situations that make them uncomfortable.

KEEP TABS ON YOUR CHILD

It should be natural for parents to want to know their child's whereabouts and activities that they frequently participate in to ensure their safety. Maintaining a connection and staying informed about their daily routines can help parents respond promptly to any potential concerns or emergencies, even if the child does not live with both parents. Parents can also include other caregivers they trust, such as a grandmother, aunt, etc., to keep tabs on the child if they cannot do so at a particular time. It is also important to balance monitoring and respecting your child's privacy.

Establish clear communication channels, and encourage open discussions about their plans, activities, and places they intend to visit (if they are 'of age'). By fostering a trusting relationship, your child is more likely to share their whereabouts and keep you informed voluntarily. Also, set expectations regarding curfews, permissions for going out, and regular check-ins. This structure will allow you to stay informed about their activities without being overly intrusive. Leverage technology so that you can track your child's whereabouts when necessary. Use only to ensure they are safe and not intrude on their privacy. Privacy intrusion will only allow the child not to trust you and not share vital information that could put their safety at risk. It is important to balance monitoring and allowing your child to grow and develop their independence, fostering trust while keeping their safety at the forefront of your priorities.

Chapter Fourteen

Mandatory Reporting

According to data provided by Wikipedia, the number of hotline calls related to child abuse and neglect has experienced a significant increase over the years. In 1963, the reported number of calls stood at 150,000, surging to approximately 3.3 million in 2009 nationwide. The volume of calls received annually is estimated to be around 3.6 million, indicating a substantial demand for support and assistance. This translates to an average of 9,000 calls per day or 63,000 per week, highlighting the alarming prevalence of child abuse and its impact on families.

Mandatory reporting laws legally obligate individuals with regular contact with vulnerable populations, including children, disabled people, and senior citizens, to immediately report any suspected or disclosed abuse or mistreatment. These laws ensure that professionals and individuals in specific roles are responsible for protecting those who cannot protect themselves. Various professionals are typically mandated to report incidents of abuse or mistreatment. For instance, educators such as teachers, principals, and school personnel play a vital role in identifying and reporting potential cases of abuse within the school setting. Social workers, nurses, doctors, and other healthcare workers are also professionals legally required to report any suspicions or disclosures of abuse.

It is important to note that mandatory reporting laws vary across jurisdictions, and the specific roles and professionals covered may differ. The exact reporting requirements and procedures may also vary, including the designated authorities or agencies to which reports must be made. It is key that a person checks with the laws of their jurisdiction to get more information on mandatory reporting specific to where they reside.

Mandatory reporting laws help safeguard vulnerable populations and ensure that intervention and support are provided promptly by legally obligating certain professionals to report suspected abuse. These laws underscore the collective responsibility to protect and advocate for those at risk of harm, including sexual abuse, and emphasize the importance of early intervention in promoting their safety and well-being.

The enforcement of mandatory reporting laws holds individuals accountable for their role in reporting abuse and promotes a culture of vigilance and responsibility. These laws serve as a deterrent to those who may otherwise pay no heed to mistreatment or abuse, emphasizing a collective duty to protect those most vulnerable in society.

Mandatory reporting laws often provide legal protections for individuals who report in good faith. These protections are in place to encourage reporting and to alleviate concerns about potential repercussions for those who fulfill their duty to report suspicions or evidence of abuse. While mandatory reporting laws are vital to safeguarding vulnerable populations, it is essential to recognize that reporting alone is not a solution to the complex issue of sexual abuse. It is equally important to ensure that appropriate support systems are in place for victims and that investigations and interventions are carryout out sensitively and effectively.

CONCLUSION

My entire being was violated by the presence of outsiders, casting a long, haunting shadow over a significant part of my childhood. At one point, the memories of their transgressions etched deeply within me, stained my innocence, and left behind a legacy of darkness and despair. The experiences of all three perpetrators had a profound and lasting impact on my life. The darkness they introduced to my childhood reverberated throughout my earlier existence, leaving me with a deep-seated trauma and a shattered sense of identity. The pain and anguish I endured impaired my being, an ever-present reminder of the depths human cruelty can reach.

It is crucial to acknowledge that healing from the trauma of sexual abuse is a deeply individualized process that unfolds at its own pace. Each survivor's journey is unique, shaped by many factors, such as the nature and duration of the abuse, their resilience, and the available support systems. Recognize that a child's healing timeline may differ from what is anticipated and the importance of respecting their process. A child may experience intense emotions, fear, anger, or sadness. As a parent, it is essential to remain steadfast in supporting the child, offering a safe and non-judgmental space for the child to express their feelings.

The recognition of the profound impact of sexual abuse on a child's life demands a parental response that is both sensitive and proactive. As a parent, your role in supporting your child's healing and recovery cannot be overstated. By embracing patience, understanding, and seeking professional support, you can navigate this intricate journey with effectiveness and compassion. Professional support can play a vital role in a child's healing process. Seeking guidance from therapists and counselors with expertise in trauma and abuse can provide valuable tools and strategies for both child and parent. These professionals can help victims navigate emotional challenges and develop coping mechanisms. They can also guide parents in navigating their child's healing and recovery process.

If a child has experienced sexual abuse, communicate openly and honestly, letting the child know that you are there for them unconditionally. Encourage the child to share their feelings and experiences at their own pace, without judgment or pressure. Offer reassurance, validation, and support, emphasizing that they are not alone. Encourage self-care and self-expression. Help the child to explore coping mechanisms that resonate with them, such as engaging in creative outlets, physical activities, or mindfulness practices.

Advocate for your child's needs and rights. Understand that your role as a parent includes advocating for your child's well-being, both within your family and in larger contexts such as their school and community. Be prepared to converse with teachers, administrators, and other relevant individuals to ensure your child's needs are met and feel safe and supported in all aspects of their life.

Seek professional help from therapists, counselors, or specialized organizations that have experience working with survivors of sexual abuse. Additionally, educate yourself on the impacts of child sexual abuse and the recovery process, maintain open lines of communication with your child, embrace patience, take care of your well-being, and remember it is not your fault. Your dedication and commitment as a parent are instrumental in helping your child overcome the effects of child sexual abuse and reclaim their lives. Remember, your child will need you now more than ever.

It is crucial that parents and caregivers sought after education about the effects of child sexual abuse, understand the grooming behavior of perpetrators, how to cope with child sexual abuse, and how to minimize the risk of child sexual abuse. They should familiarize themselves with support organizations, hotlines, and community resources that specialize in assisting survivors of sexual abuse. Being knowledgeable about available resources will help to provide children with appropriate guidance and connect them and their families with the help they may need.

It is also very important to know the behaviors children may exhibit when enduring the trauma of sexual abuse. Some of these include nightmares or fear of being alone at night, decreased interest in school activities, self-harm behaviors such as cutting wrists, stomachaches, headaches, mood swings, and changes in eating habits. Other behavioral changes include shyness to remove clothing when it is time for a bath, bleeding in the vaginal area, thumb sucking, and bedwetting. Some children may become sexually aggressive, unafraid to discuss sexual topics, or may need to expose themselves inappropriately. We all bear a responsibility to protect the well-being of children. If you have reason to believe that a child is experiencing abuse, it is vital to contact your local authorities immediately. By reporting your concerns and allowing the appropriate authorities to intervene, you can play a pivotal role in ensuring the safety and welfare of that vulnerable child. Your support and advocacy can make a profound difference in their life.

Mandatory reporting laws establish a legally enforceable duty for individuals with contact with vulnerable populations to report suspected or confirmed mistreatment or abuse to the authorities. These laws play a fundamental role in safeguarding those who may be unable to protect themselves, including victims of sexual abuse, and emphasize the collective responsibility we have in ensuring their safety and well-being. By promoting reporting, these laws help prevent further harm and facilitate timely intervention, ultimately creating a safer and more protective environment for vulnerable individuals.

May my story stand as a testament to the resilience of survivors, a reminder that healing is possible even in the wake of unimaginable pain. Let it be an invitation of empathy, understanding, and support for all who bear the weight of such a violation. May we shatter the silence and create a world where no one's core is breached and where the harmonious whispers of healing and restoration replace the echoes of violation.

REFERENCES

https://victimsofcrime.org/

https://www.rainn.org/warning-signs

https://bjs.ojp.gov/

https://www.americanbar.org/groups/public_interest/child_law/resources/child_law_practiceonline/child_law_practice/vol-34/november-2015/understanding-sexual-grooming-in-child-abuse-cases/

https://nij.ojp.gov/library/publications/national-institute-justice-annual-report-2003

http://unh.edu/ccrc/

https://en.wikipedia.org/wiki/Mandatory_reporting_in_the_United_States

www.ingramcontent.com/pod-product-compliance
Lightning Source LLC
LaVergne TN
LVHW010925110826
845149LV00013B/2486

* 9 7 8 1 9 5 7 8 0 9 5 8 8 *